*f*P

MegaChange

How Today's Leading Companies Have Transformed Their Workforces

William F. Joyce

Amos Tuck School, Dartmouth College

THE FREE PRESS

THE FREE PRESS
A Division of Simon & Schuster Inc.
1230 Avenue of the Americas
New York, NY 10020

Designed by MM Design 2000 Inc.

Manufactured in the United States of America

10 9 8 7 6 5 4 3 2 1

Library of Congress Cataloging-in-Publication Data

Joyce, William F.
    MegaChange : how today's leading companies have transformed their
workforces / William F. Joyce.
        p.   cm.
    1. Organizational change.   2. Organizational effectiveness.
I. Title.
HD58.8.J69   1999   99-27981   CIP
658.4'06—dc21

ISBN 0-684-85625-5

This book is dedicated to my parents

Franklyn Willingham Joyce
and
Mary Abigail Lucas Joyce

from whom I learned the values that form the foundation for this book

And to my wife

Linda Marie Azman Joyce

whose integrity, compassion and professionalism embody the
managerial commitment that it will take to enact its ideas

And to my son

Jeffrey William Joyce

who provided the inspiration for the creation of organizations
such as those described here

Contents

Preface

This is a book about organizations and organizational change. It represents my thinking on a topic that has occupied most of my career as an academic and consultant. It is rooted in a diverse set of academic literatures and practical experiences that I think distinguish my perspective from others that can more easily be associated with particular schools of thought and practice. It is fundamentally both eclectic and integrative, and I hope reflects an organizational reality that is too often fragmented by conventional theory and practice.

This is also a book about theory for practice. It is commonplace to hear from practitioners that they find most organizational research to be irrelevant, misinformed, or impractical. Similarly, many academics regard management practice in large-scale transformation as a dangerous art, lacking in theoretical foundation and practiced without regard to the actual merits of the methodologies employed. But unlike my colleagues who line up on one or the other side of this argument, I believe that a solution to this critical problem involves recognizing the merits of both positions.

What we need is relevant theory that addresses the real problems of large-scale organizational change. I do not believe that this theory can be found in any one discipline or managerial practice; it is eclectic in nature, and must be integrated to be useful. This book attempts just such an integration. It draws selectively from the academic literatures of strategic management, organizational science, humanistic psychology, and military strategy and then attempts to integrate these ideas into a cohesive model of large-scale organizational change and transformation. This integration is based upon my personal experience as an academic consultant in organizational change over the past twenty-five years.

During this journey I have been fortunate to have several mentors. First and foremost among these is Jay Galbraith. Jay and I worked together at the Wharton School in the early days of my career, and we have remained close friends and collaborators ever since. His work has been inspirational for its clarity, practicality, academic integrity, and impact.

I joined the faculty at the Amos Tuck School in 1983 to teach with James Brian Quinn in the strategy area. It was from Brian that I really received my education in strategy. His ideas have been a major influence on my thinking.

John Slocum launched me on my academic career. His enthusiasm for organizational research was contagious, and I owe him a great debt for his continuing friendship, energy and collaboration.

Lawrence Hrebiniak of the Wharton School encouraged and inspired my interest in organizational theory. Larry's academic prowess, intellectual capacity, and practical interests model what every academic strives for but rarely achieves. My work with him in strategy implementation embodies the finest sense of the term collaboration and colleagueship.

This work has also been influenced by a number of other researchers and colleagues. I am indebted to Chris Argyris, Ben Schneider, Lawrence James, Andrew Van de Ven, Paul Lawrence, Ray Miles, and Charles Snow. The early work of Kurt Lewin, Roger Barker, Victor Thompson, and James D. Thompson has been very influential.

I have also been fortunate to have had significant involvements in a number of major organizational change efforts, including those at Lucent Technologies, CitiGroup, PricewaterhouseCoopers, General Electric, Aetna, Allied-Signal, Upjohn, Ciba-Geigy and numerous other organizations. I owe a debt of gratitude to the managers of these organizations for helping me to understand the real challenges that they face in managing organizational change.

It is customary to say that although I am indebted to those above, the responsibility for this work rests squarely with the author. I am pleased to accept this responsibility. Writing this book has provided me with an opportunity to speak about organizational and consulting practices that I believe to be wrong, faddish, misinformed and, ultimately, dangerous and unethical. It has also required me to say something constructive about how the real problems that these methods are used to address, *should* be addressed. Undoubtedly, due to the complexity of the issues, I have made mistakes in my analyses. For these I apologize. However, I hope that the spirit with which these ideas have been taken up is appreciated. I believe that we will not be able to change our large institutions effectively and ethically without both theory and practice, and without knowledge of both how *and* why. This integration is what this book attempts, and against which it should be evaluated.

Setting the Stage

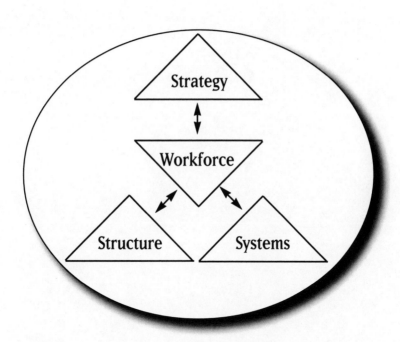

CHAPTER 1

The Model

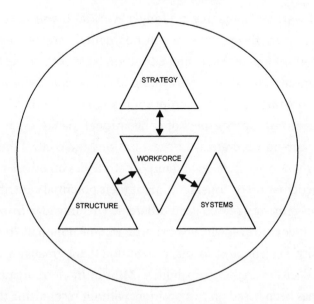

This is a book about organizations and organizational change. Specifically, it is a book about creating organizations that engage, liberate, and develop their human potential to the greatest extent possible, and in so doing achieve unprecedented levels of productivity and satisfaction. Thus far, our organizations, their managers, and the academics and consultants who advise them have not done a very good job at this. This book attempts to show where and why we have failed and, more important, what we can do about it. We can no longer afford organizations that lack vision and direction, that confuse and obstruct progress with useless systems and procedures, that bury creativity in bureaucracy, and that deny workers' needs for meaningful work and careers. Yet this is precisely what is happening and will continue to happen if we do not begin changing our institutions now.

MegaChange

The old ways of managing no longer work and will never work again. They are flawed in a most fundamental way. Management practice, thinking, research, and education have been erected on an insubstantial foundation—*the assumption of human limitations as a basis for organizing.* This assumption is so pervasive that it can be found in almost every aspect of conventional managing, from the way we over-bureaucratize our organizations and control the workforce to the way we develop and impose strategies on others without their participation or consideration of their potential contribution.

Management research is no different. The only idea from organization theory to ever win a Nobel prize was the notion of "bounded rationality,"[1] essentially a formal recognition that humans are limited in their decision-making capabilities. Most of modern organization theory has been based on this position, without recognizing that just as people have limitations, they also have capabilities. *MegaChange* is the name I use in this book to describe a process of organizational transformation that is based on assumptions of human *capability* instead of human limitations. Of course, humans have both capabilities and limitations, but I believe that we have a great deal to gain from a different starting point. There are some obvious advantages to this approach.

First, *it puts people back into organizations.* Certainly, we have talked a lot about this, but our success has been less than admirable, as outlined above. We have implemented "programs" that purport to empower, involve, and engage people differently, but we have never really changed our fundamental assumptions about the role that people can play. For the most part we have had a "surface" effect. Things look different but really aren't. We reengineer until it is

4

management's turn to be reengineered, de-layer until we really have to trust people, and debureaucratize with process staffs and quality experts instead of the people who really do the work. These inconsistencies are due to the fact that our methods are changing but our assumptions are not. Assuming a capable workforce means that its members may have something valid to say about reengineering management, that they can be trusted, and that they can play as important a role in debureaucratizing as specialized staffs of quality experts.

Second, *assumptions of capability suggest a higher standard for organizational performance.* Many firms are obsessed with financial performance, but most people do not get up in the morning to make earnings per share. They get up and go to work to take care of their family, to utilize their skills, to achieve something that they could not achieve alone. These are personally meaningful tasks that have no equivalent counterpart in most organizational strategies or missions. Many aspects of meaningful accomplishment are vague, nonquantitative, and impossible to capture with financial measures. Financial performance measures are important because they provide some of the information necessary to gauge our performance. But often we mistake the measure for the meaning. We need to remember that these measures are not the real performance; they are merely imperfect indicators of it. Real performance is human.

Meaning, productivity, and financial performance go hand in hand. Work cannot be meaningful if it is not productive. However, the converse is not true. We can be somewhat productive while performing nonmeaningful work. I think we all know that. We can pay people enough, or threaten them enough, or extort their contribution enough to achieve productivity even when the things that we are asking them to do are not valued by them. We achieve "productivity," but it is a weak cousin of what really is possible.

Real productivity is achieved by accomplishing things that are of value not only to the organization but also to the person performing the work. We have overemphasized the former and underemphasized the latter. We realize meaning by doing and accomplishing things that are consistent with our values. This fundamental concept—meaning through action that is consistent with values—has been recognized in philosophy[2] and psychology[3] for hundreds of years, but it has yet to find its way into management practice in a significant way. Most corporate strategies are devoid of substantial human content and values. But without it, why should anyone care about the innocuous words crafted into a mission statement by a few people who supposedly represent an entire organization? Why should *their* goals be *my* goals?

We can have productivity without meaningful work, but we probably cannot have flexibility, satisfaction, adaptability, and *radically higher* productivity. These require human engagement and not disaffection, and this requires meaningful work—work in which we care about the outcomes. Work that has human content. Assumptions of human limitations lead to management practices and actions that exclude, deny, even organize away precisely the type of human engagement that is necessary for future success. Simply focusing on productivity and excluding the broader context of workforce values and meaning results in achieving precisely too little of what we set out in search of in the first place—productivity. It is too simple an idea for a very complex situation.

What Is *MegaChange*?

MegaChange means designing and transforming organizations based on assumptions of human capability rather than limitations, using all the tools and principles available to us from management practice and theory. It is a new and different starting point. It prescribes a different journey. Along the way it implies different perspectives about how to change organizations. These perspectives are derived from the diverse literatures of management, organization theory, military strategy, and psychology, and all are related to the

Table 1.1
What is *MegaChange*?

MegaChange *Is*:	MegaChange *Is Not*:
Capability focused	Limitations focused
Transformation	Transition
Systemwide	Piecemeal
Cultural	Mechanistic
Empowering	Controlling
Concepts, actions, and tools	Tools without concepts
Theory *for* practice	Theory *or* practice
Reformation	Mere reengineering, restructuring

fundamental assumption of capability. Basing organizations on the capability assumption lets us see the fundamental ideas about organizations in a new and different way, and as a consequence we can integrate them into an alternative model of transformation (see Table 1.1). These different perspectives on organizations are taken up one by one in the chapters that follow.

MegaChange is a total systemwide cultural transformation of the organization. *MegaChange* affects everyone in the organization and results in new and changed ways of thinking, acting, and cooperating. *MegaChange* is not restructuring or reengineering, and it is not a mere transition. *MegaChange* is produced using an integrated set of concepts, actions, and tools that are based upon assumptions of human capability rather than limitations. *MegaChange* results in a joint optimization of organizational and individual performance, capability and satisfaction.

The Need for *MegaChange*

Faulty assumptions require a new approach to organizing and organizational change. But why is this change so urgent now? A partial answer to this question is that the magnitude of environmental, competitive, and global market change we are experiencing is unprecedented. These changes are documented in a number of recent books that make this point passionately.[4,5,6] A more complete answer recognizes that we cannot address these new challenges with more of the same old management solutions applied in larger and larger doses.

Organizations have spent billions in the last decade in attempts to improve productivity and effectiveness. Statistics indicate that from 1990 to 1995, 85 percent of U.S.-based corporations engaged in some variety of restructuring.[7] Of these, 60 percent report that they did not get the productivity gains that they wanted from the change effort. And 44 percent say that things actually got worse! Work satisfaction decreased in 80 percent of the firms. Having failed at change, and with nothing new to guide them, 68 percent of these organizations restructured again within one year. These are terrifying statistics. Results for reengineering efforts are only slightly better.[8]

Most of the changes in management practice are just the same old things done under new guises and dressed up in new clothes. As March and Simon noted, "Not so much new has been said in management," but it has "been said over and over again in a variety of languages."[9] We need a new direction and new solutions that are uniquely compatible with the capability assumption and contextual changes in competition, technology, and workforce values, as described below.

Hypercompetition and Technological Revolution

We are witnessing the birth of what my colleague Richard D'Aveni calls "hypercompetition,"[10] a state in which the rate of change in the competitive rules of the game are in such flux that only the most adaptive, fleet, and nimble organizations will survive. In this world, competitive advantages must constantly be reinvented, and organization becomes the fundamental source of distinctive competence.[11] And we are participating in this change on a global scale. There is a relentless emphasis on cost competition, and quality—once the "holy grail" in many industries—is now expected by consumers and is ceasing to be a point of differentiation. We want it quicker, we want it cheaper, and we want it "our way." Is this the same level of competition that we faced even ten years ago? Many believe that there has been a fundamental quantitative and qualitative shift in competition that is requiring organizational change on an unprecedented scale.

Technology is revolutionizing society, and while many of the changes were predicted earlier,[12] the actual *experience* of these changes is startling. When I started my first career as an aerospace engineer in 1968, work was being done with analog computers, and a mechanical office calculator that could compute a square root was both costly and impressive. Today we can place the computing power of an entire 1970s university computing center on someone's desk, and our ability to productively utilize this power seems inexhaustible. New forms of electronic networking such as the Internet are allowing nearly instantaneous communication and problem solving without any geographical constraints. Flexible manufacturing is fundamentally changing the way products are produced and firms are organized. The new manufacturing firm is more democratic, less hierarchical, and less bureaucratic. As basic work is performed by "smart" robots in increasingly integrated production facilities, the workers that were once the "line" become the "staff" that supports more and more sophisticated technology. Fewer and fewer lower-skilled tasks are performed by humans, freeing them for more challenging work that requires higher and higher skill levels. Manufacturing organizations, once the bastion of bureaucracy, are increasingly finding that they have to transform themselves into radically new organizational forms.

The Values Imperative

In the midst of these changes in competition and technology, the most dramatic shifts have taken place in workforce values. In fact, it is these shifts, more than anything else, which are causing organizations to search for new and more human ways of increasing productivity and competitiveness. Recent surveys confirm that for the first time personal lives and family are more important than careers to a majority of workers.[13] And people are expecting and demanding that organizations recognize these preferences. Twenty years ago less than 5 percent of the workforce expected to find satisfaction at work. Statistics today indicate that 40 percent of employees see self-fulfillment as a fundamental right of employment.[14] And many organizations, in trying to cope with changes in technology and competition, are implementing organizations that fail to recognize these fundamental shifts in values. The consequence: disaffection, disloyalty, and defection.

A New Direction

The changes in competition, technology, and workforce values should make every reader of this book uneasy. We cannot cope with changes in competition and technology as we have in the past. What worked before will never work again. The era of "more of the same" is past. It is time for real innovation and transformation in organizations. Managing in the future will not mean expecting people to do more with less, and then *demanding* that they do so. The "values imperative" has ended all that forever. It complicates the problem considerably.

We *must* be more competitive, but now we must do it in a way that recognizes the desire—perhaps the demand—for meaningful and valuable work, the recognition of family, and personal satisfaction. The old way—not just in old-fashioned management thinking but in current efforts to de-layer, downsize, and reengineer—was to require compliance and reward those that made the sacrifice and punish those that would not. We extracted performance from some, but without engaging the whole person. Workers that did not respond to these demands were either downsized or relegated to marginal positions, denying organizations access to their potential contributions and needed collaboration. We acted in a way that was consistent with our core assumptions of human limitations—assumptions that now must be discarded for a more optimistic perspective.

The implications are clear. People are expecting and demanding a higher quality of life, and those demands reach into the workplace.[15] Many organizations are ignoring rather than embracing these changes in values.[16] The consequence is lower rather than higher performance. The desired changes are changes in the direction of workforce empowerment, with individual and family values being seen as important as the organizational goal of productivity. Workers are demanding that the workplace provide opportunities for achievement and satisfaction, and they are not willing to settle for a job that only provides the means for obtaining satisfaction elsewhere.

Values are constraining the viable directions of change for organizations. Changes that attempt to obtain higher productivity and competitiveness and that do not accommodate the values imperative will not succeed. Rethinking this concept is no longer just a nice idea or something "we'll get around to." It is something we have to do and have to do now. Values are shaping the direction of organizational evolution and requiring that firms adopt new, engaging, and more human ways of competing, not only because they are appealing, but also because they are necessary.

Meeting the Challenge

The vast majority of current transformation efforts are doomed to failure. Without really believing in the capability assumption discussed above, and without understanding that the values imperative requires a fundamental rethinking of organization design and transformation, we have looked for quick-fix answers to our problems. Consequently we have failed to embrace the fact that fundamental change must occur in organizations—in their strategies, structures, systems, and workforce—if we are to succeed. *Everything* must change in a logical, consistent, and mutually supporting way. We have treated transformation as a localized activity. We have expected radical changes in productivity with minimal interventions in organizations. We have laid the burden of change on the backs of the workers when it is *management* that has the most to do.

This has occurred for a number of reasons. Obviously, it is easier to ask others to change than to change ourselves. But there is another, more subtle and perhaps more pervasive, reason. Management history is littered with "fads" like "Management by Objectives," "Matrix Management," "Sensitivity Training and T-Groups," and, more recently, ideas like "Core Competence," "Total Quality Management," and "Empowerment." Even fringe ideas like transactional analysis and transcendental meditation found their way into mainstream organizations at one time or another.

Each of these approaches has had some obvious merits, and many, like Management by Objectives and Matrix Management, have become essential elements in management practice. But at their beginning, all were marked by an overcommitment to their concepts from the management community that was significantly out of proportion to what they had to offer. I remember clearly when at the height of the interest in Matrix, my colleague Jay Galbraith and I would frequently be asked by a major client to "Matrix" them. When we advised that it didn't make sense for their strategic situation, they would implore us to help them anyway. Others were doing it, and they wanted it done to them too!

The reason for this is simple. Ever since the beginning of systematic management thinking we have been looking for the "one best way."[17] And although everything points to the fact that there is no such thing, we have refused to abandon the search! Now, as we grapple with the changes discussed above, our search becomes even more fervent, and we become more and more committed to finding the "answer." And we have chosen to focus our search on the workforce rather than on our organizations themselves.

This focus is both understandable and misplaced. It is understandable because the workforce is the locus of the values changes that are causing us to rethink management. It is misplaced because, as the discussion above shows, competition and technology are forcing change in strategy, structures, and systems as well. It is the interaction of the workforce and the organizations in which they are imbedded that matters.

Our response has been a little like what philosophers call the "fallacy of the drunkard's search."[18] When observed peering at the ground beneath a streetlight on a darkened street, the drunkard is asked what he is doing. He replies that he is searching for his car keys, which he has lost. Where did he lose them? Somewhere down the street, he replies. But why, then, are you searching here? Because this is where the light is, he replies.

It is easiest for us to look for solutions at the workforce level because that is where the light is. It doesn't threaten management's values; indeed, it may even cater to them. We are, after all, doing something good when we allow workers a greater say. And we even know something about how to do it. We have had the previous experience of the "Human Relations" movement, "Participative Management," "Quality of Worklife" efforts, and "Employee Involvement" to guide us. The fact that none of these has ever lived up to its potential doesn't seem to tip us off that we are searching under the streetlight rather than where the problem is. The point is simple: there can be no solution to our complex problems without addressing the organization as a whole. This means fundamentally reexamining our systems, structures, and strategies and changing them in a direction that engages, liberates, facilitates, and develops human capacity and

Figure 1.1
The *MegaChange* Model

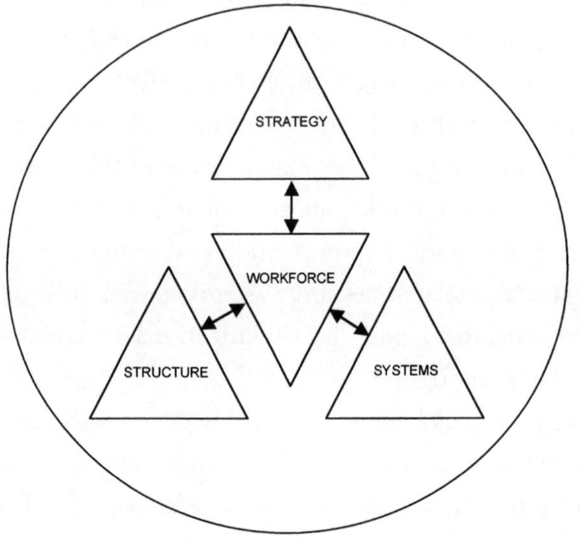

productivity. Hoping for a simple solution to the monumental challenges we are now facing is inconsistent with the bulk of management theory, and with common sense as well.

What is needed, then, is a way of thinking about organizations and change that does not lead us to focus exclusively on any one element of organization design. Fortunately, we have several very useful perspectives to help us with this.[19,20,21] The specific model developed for this book—the *MegaChange* model—is illustrated in Figure 1.1. As we shall see, the model is similar to earlier approaches in some respects, and very different from them in others. The framework is very important to this book because it is used to organize everything that follows.

The *MegaChange* Model

The *MegaChange* model has four main action components: *empowering the workforce, engaging systems, reforming structures,* and *remaking strategy.* Each element of this model and the important interactions among them will be discussed in detail in the chapters that follow. However, we need an overview here to allow us to focus on the aspects of this approach that, building on the capability assumption, are quite different from other perspectives.

Empowering the Workforce

The first element of the model is the workforce. In earlier approaches it has usually been referred to as the "people" component of the various models. The meaning here is similar, and the workforce component includes the concepts, actions, and tools for targeting, stimulating, and creating an empowered workforce. This component of the model is what most efforts at empowerment, in all of its guises, have focused on.

The Human Relations movement, Quality of Worklife efforts, Employee Involvement, and most other change programs have addressed this component of the model to the exclusion of the other components. These earlier approaches are vital to understanding this component of the model, but are not in and of themselves capable of producing the levels of performance, human engagement, productivity, and satisfaction that are now called for. Transformation requires that all of the elements of the model build upon and support one another in a complex pattern of change. Changing one and only one element is a *transition,* not a transformation. Moreover, the sequence in which the elements are changed is critical. Each of the remaining three components and the interactions among them must be part of a carefully orchestrated sequence of change.

Engaging Systems

As organizations attempt to reinvent themselves, one of the first barriers that they encounter are their systems. In this model, "systems" refers to the processes used to manage the organization. Many of these refer in some way or another to the human resource systems of the organization. In particular, many of the most significant problems in creating highly effective organizations revolve around performance appraisal and reward systems and the ways that careers are managed. What current transformation efforts fail to recognize is that most of our systems are historical: they are for the most part relics from the past that impede rather than nurture and further change. The older approaches are preoccupied with control rather than creativity, contribution, and engagement. *Engaging systems* are quite different: they liberate, access, and respond to the potential for human contribution, and in so doing, they encourage change and adaptability and enable organizations to react with speed, flexibility, and competence. This portion of the model is focused on the concepts, actions, and tools that are necessary for this more enlightened purpose.

Reforming Structures

Recent years have witnessed an unprecedented level of change in organizational structures. And while these changes have in some cases produced short-run improvements in productivity, they have devastated our ability to maintain these gains in the long run. The initial "solutions" that were employed emphasized two things: complexity and costs. We responded to changes in technology and markets with more complex structures, and to the need to do things more cheaply by taking people out of the organization. In the latter case this meant massive and unprecedented downsizing, "right"-sizing, de-layering, and, in many cases, the destruction of our human capability.

These efforts did not have the desired effect. Now, we are becoming more thoughtful in reinventing our conceptions of what constitutes appropriate spans of control and levels of hierarchy. We are rethinking the role of teams and teamwork. These changes are occurring hand in hand with changes in information technology and human resource systems, and they must work together more closely than ever before. Organizations are de-layering, shedding old and useless rules, and becoming more horizontal and process focused.

Generally, these things mean less structure rather than more, and require the total involvement of the entire workforce. This engagement is not possible in organizations that have discarded their human resources to achieve lower costs, for the people that remain understand their true role in such corporations. Debureaucratization should not mean dehumanization as it has too often in the past. *Reforming structures* refers to the structural concepts, actions, and tools necessary for creating organizations that achieve unprecedented levels of productivity and satisfaction by engaging human capability rather than denying it.

Remaking Strategy

The concept of strategy has been central to management thinking for centuries, beginning with the military strategy literature. Strategic planning, and the planning culture that supported it, was a major part of management education in the 1980s. Major consulting practices sprang from it, and organizations felt incomplete without a planning department using all the newest tools and techniques. Yet something was missing, and for the most part it is still missing today. Organizations attempted to substitute strategic planning for strategic thinking, and strategy became the province of planners and not doers. Over time many notable planning efforts withered and died as planning activities became more and more isolated from the businesses they were created to serve. Strategy was then moved away from planning staffs, and back into the hands of line managers who could no longer afford to abdicate this crucial aspect of their responsibilities.

This step was positive. But corporate strategies are only *barely* living up to the critical role that they must play in tomorrow's corporations. The essential criteria for future strategies will be the extent to which they engender motivation and commitment in an empowered workforce and how well they facilitate coordination and cooperation in de-layered, less bureaucratic, and more "boundaryless" organizations. Traditional means of control will be impossible, and strategy will play a key role in uniting an organization's efforts behind objectives that inspire motivation and commitment rather than demanding and extracting it. Common understanding of strategy and vision will allow unity of effort in situations where no rule exists to legislate it and no hierarchy is there to enforce it.

An effective strategy is one that engages human potential rather than denying it. Financial objectives dominate corporate strategies, but people do not get up in the morning to make "earnings per share." Individuals seek meaning and accomplishment from work. They are attracted to organizations that have created a vision and purpose that allow them to accomplish something larger than what they could ever hope to achieve alone, and that stands for something they can believe in. Most strategies are emasculated, devoid of human content, and meaningless. They are produced behind closed doors and "communicated" to people who are expected to embrace them. There is little genuine participation in the process of creating them, even though it is often the participation process itself that makes strategy meaningful.

Remaking strategy refers to the concepts, actions, and tools necessary for producing strategies that develop human motivation, commitment, and coordination. Remaking strategy makes work meaningful, allows achievement through collaboration, and develops consensus around vision. It goes far beyond current practices that relegate strategy to upper echelons in the firm, that embrace empowerment only to achieve higher productivity, and that believe that strategy is first formulated and then merely communicated to workers who embrace ideals developed by others without their participation.

Features of This Book

The remaining chapters of this book develop the *MegaChange* model and the arguments supporting it. Each chapter follows a consistent logic, which adheres to two major features. The first is a linking of concepts, actions, and tools for *MegaChange* in a consistent framework. The second is the use of analytical examples from practice.

Concepts, Actions, and Tools

Unlike other books on change, *MegaChange* is practice-driven and theory-based. All other books are either one or the other. In this book concepts are linked to critical change actions, and then to specific tools for their implementation. The result is that managers understand why these actions are essential and also how, specifically, to implement them.

Each chapter begins with a discussion of the major principles or concepts that drive change activities at that stage of the transformation process. As discussed above, these concepts are derived from management theory and practice, organizational theory, military and business strategy, and psychology. The capability assumption of *MegaChange* directs our attention to a different set of concepts than those used in conventional models of change like reengineering and restructuring.

Each concept is then systematically related to a set of actions. These actions are similar to "critical success factors" for change: each one must be successfully accomplished for the transformation to proceed to the next level. Failing at even one can endanger the whole effort. Making things even more challenging is the fact that most actions must be accomplished before moving on to the next stage of transformation. The actions are therefore individually necessary, but not individually sufficient for accomplishing change. All or a substantial portion of them must be achieved before change at the next level can be successful.

Finally, each chapter presents a set of tools for implementing the actions derived from the concepts and the capability assumption. Some of these are sophisticated, highly developed methods for achieving transformation. As we near the end of the book and enter largely uncharted waters, these tools become somewhat more tentative. In every chapter, however, I attempt to link concepts, actions, and tools for change within the overall model of *MegaChange* that is at the heart of this book.

Analytical Examples

The ideas for *MegaChange* were born in practice as well as in theory, and are well grounded. I wish to establish credibility for the ideas by connecting them to companies and work that has been very visible in the media, as well as by their foundations in management theory. However, I do not intend to use these examples as simple illustrations of "best practices." The examples are analytical as opposed to illustrative. Philosophers distinguish between three kinds of knowledge: knowledge of, knowledge why, and knowledge how. Best practices represent only one of the three kinds of knowing about change—knowledge of what others have done, or knowledge of. The impossibility of such a simple-minded approach to change management is obvious, no matter how much effort is devoted to it. It will be impossible to meet the challenges of hypercompetition without also having knowledge of why and how. I therefore do not simply repeat examples from practice; I analyze them in terms of the concepts, actions, and tools necessary to understand why and how successful change can be produced. It is interesting to see how change is managed at Motorola, Intel, or Microsoft—but it is far more important to understand the general theory and practice of large-scale transformation.

Each chapter utilizes examples to analyze change efforts in the following way. After introducing the core concepts, actions, and tools for the chapter, I will *analyze and critique well-known change efforts* in terms of these ideas. This will illustrate both the strengths and weaknesses of these efforts and provide a connection and insight into leading practice for the reader. Following this critical application of the ideas, the chapter will end with a *detailed and specific analysis of a positive example* of the application of these concepts. Developing this type of analytical framework should allow the reader to apply the concepts, actions, and tools of each chapter in the more important context of their own organizations and change initiatives.

Most of the major examples are based upon my first-hand experiences in the organizations being discussed. I want the examples to create a sense of being on the inside of the change for the reader, as well as to illustrate the major concepts of the chapter. *MegaChange* is based on the explicit assumption of human capability rather than limitations, as discussed above. To be consistent with this position, all of the major examples are positive, and the organizations that are described are exceptional. Change efforts that are profiled are drawn from Lucent, Citicorp, Price Waterhouse, and a major defense contractor. There were many examples of failures that I could have drawn upon to make the points that I need to make, but I am choosing to make my arguments on the basis of the strength of my major examples rather than their weaknesses.

Organization of This Book

The book is organized into three major segments, as follows:

Segment I: Setting the Stage

This segment includes Chapters 1 and 2. Chapter 1 introduced the book, its basic organization, and the core model. It has also discussed why organizations are changing, and some likely directions for this change. Chapter 2, "The Evolution of Adaptive Organizations," puts these changes in context by tracing the development of new forms of organizations. The newest form of management—Adaptive Organizations—are described as "Stage III" organizations—ones that have moved beyond Bureaucracy (Stage I) and excessively Complex (Stage II) forms. Whereas Complex structures got things done by violating principles of management (by creating things like Matrix management), Stage III Adaptive Organizations accomplish unprecedented levels of productivity and satisfaction by reinventing these principles.

The core characteristics of Adaptive Organizations are derived from my own field research in many organizations and are presented at the end of Chapter 2, along with specific behavioral descriptions for each aspect of these new organizational cultures. It is hoped that this will make each concept more concrete and personally meaningful to the reader.

Segment II: *MegaChange*

Segment II is composed of Chapters 3 through 6, each of which presents one of the core stages of the *MegaChange* model presented in Figure 1.1. The logical order of the chapters corresponds to the actual sequence of change that would be followed in attempting to implement these ideas. Which of these chapters seems most relevant to your organization is one rough gauge of how far you have come in implementing these ideas. In my consulting, I have noticed that people are much more comfortable and skillful at implementing the ideas contained in Chapter 3, "Empowering the Workforce," than they are with the concepts presented in the later chapters. Some have successfully debureaucratized as described in Chapter 5, but virtually none have reached the level described in Chapter 6, "Remaking Strategy."

The order and content of these chapters is as follows. Chapter 3 deals with "empowering the workforce." The central argument of the chapter is that this must be the first step in transformation because the magnitude and difficulty of the problems being addressed demand the involvement and contribution of everyone in the organization. No manager or management team can hope to be smart enough to create the types of organizations that are needed without the legitimate involvement of everyone in the organization, at all levels. The foolishness of pretending that we can is readily apparent in hypercompetitive environments. The ideas of the chapter are illustrated using the Lucent GROWS Cultural Transformation as an example. This is a major effort that is just beginning and extends management practice in some new and important ways. I will analyze this transformation effort using the concepts of the *MegaChange* model, giving the reader an inside view of one of the most important change efforts in recent history.

Chapter 4, "Engaging Systems," shows how workforce empowerment efforts often stop short of real gains by becoming disengaged from actual work practices and organizational needs. Processes like reengineering and Total Quality Management are shown to violate several of the important principles of real systems change. I provide several examples of the failure of such programs in prominent companies, along with a diagnosis of the reasons for these failures using the concepts, actions, and tools from this chapter. I then introduce and analyze the Citibank Team Challenge Process as an illustration of effective change in organizational systems.

As systems change they run into structural barriers. New compensation schemes and career methods are inconsistent with old structures and levels of hierarchy. Chapter 5, "Reforming Structures," deals with the key problem of debureaucratization, or getting the "dumb stuff" out of organizations. Debureaucratization refers to efforts to reduce hierarchy, broaden spans of control, simplify rules, and organize around processes rather than functions. Major errors are being made as organizations attempt to simplify their operations. Many organizations have recently been through downsizing, restructuring, and reengineering and most have had very poor results. There is a right way to "right-size," but it is not by viewing de-layering and downsizing as isolated events in a very complex change process. After introducing the core concepts, actions, and tools for this process, the chapter will illustrate the causes for these poor results in terms of violations of *MegaChange* principles. The chapter will conclude with a detailed positive example of the application of these ideas, the Price Waterhouse Structural Transformation project. This project debureaucratized and simplified major aspects of the Price Waterhouse organization, and produced a critical emphasis on markets and revenues. It serves as a model for structural change in large, complex organizations.

An empowered workforce, changed systems, and reformed structures raise new issues for management practice. Old ideas, once held dear, are obsolete and out of place. New challenges abound. "Control without oversight" is one such challenge. Without small spans of control, how shall we manage the people we are "controlling"? With less hierarchy there will also be fewer traditional careers. How will people achieve motivation without careers? Since traditional means of coordination rely on bureaucracy, how will we achieve coordination without hierarchy?

Chapter 6, "Remaking Strategy," is a chapter for resolving these dilemmas. It proposes a new concept of strategy that goes far beyond current practices and emphasizes the human content of strategy. Without this we cannot hope for the level of engagement necessary for competing in the future. Chapter 6 develops concepts, actions, and tools for reinventing the strategy concept. Older strategic ideas are shown to be inadequate for leading new organizational forms in terms of these examples. Chapter 6 concludes the second major portion of the book.

Segment III: Achieving *MegaChange*

Segment III is composed of Chapter 7, which illustrates the overall connections among the components of the model. Each of the earlier chapters utilized a major example to illustrate the application of the concepts of the book to the specific content of that chapter. Multiple examples from Lucent, Price Waterhouse, and Citicorp were used. This chapter integrates all of the previous discussions and highlights the importance of the overall process and sequence of change activities in the context of a single large-scale change effort. This effort began with empowerment and systems change, and was followed by radical changes in the structure of the organization. Layers of hierarchy were reduced from 8 to 2, and spans of control increased from 4 to 60 in some cases. These changes are now providing the context for fundamental strategic change and are raising new challenges as the *MegaChange* process continues. Few organizations have come this far in their overall integration, consistency, and commitment to fundamental change.

Most books are either very theoretical or dominantly based in practice. This book has been designed to utilize both practical experience and relevant theory. The premise is simply that they are complementary. We need everything that we can get, and we can no longer afford to ignore either theory or practice to the detriment of the other.

CHAPTER 2

The Evolution of Adaptive Organizations

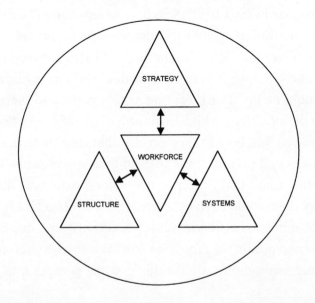

Hypercompetition, volatile technologies, and the values imperative require new approaches to organizations and change. Coping with these forces requires us to design organizations based on assumptions of human capability rather than limitations. Reducing costs is no longer the key to productivity. Revenue enhancement is the new challenge. The *MegaChange* model introduced in Chapter 1 is the mechanism for accomplishing this. The new form of organization that results is called an *adaptive organization*. Adaptive organizations replace earlier bureaucratic organizations and simplify overly complex forms of management. This chapter develops the adaptive organization concept and contrasts it with the earlier organization forms. The chapters that follow in Segment II discuss the specific concepts, actions, and tools necessary for implementing adaptive organizations using the *MegaChange* model.

The "Three Logics" of Organization Design

Designing an organization is challenging. There are many difficult change decisions that have to be made. In one of my recent consulting engagements, I faced the following situation. The firm that engaged me was struggling to implement a lateral team-based structure. Over several years they had vacillated between a traditional functional structure and a product form of organization. They would be functional for one or two years, and then adopt product divisions for a while. Each form of management had both costs and benefits. Finally, they decided that they could maximize the benefits and minimize the costs of their organization design by adopting teams that cut across the major functions of the firm. That way they would derive the benefits of functional organization (economies of scale, clear lines of authority, no duplication of effort) and product organization (focus on markets, responsiveness, quicker communication within product groups) at the same time.

However, during this time the environment that the firm faced had changed radically. Competition had intensified as several major competitors acquired other firms and now controlled larger shares of the market for my client's core products and services. Technology was changing rapidly and many of my client's systems were seriously out of date. They had downsized radically and the workforce was becoming more and more disaffected. All of the change drivers discussed in Chapter 1 were present and intensifying.

The firm faced many questions. Was the new team-based structure still appropriate in the face of these changes in competitive situation? Should they rethink their strategy before implementing the new structure? Or should they just get on with it? Compounding the problem was the fact that most of their reward systems had been developed either in the old functional form or in the product structure. The same was true of their control systems. Since the rewards and controls were developed to support two different kinds of organizations, they were not coherent and gave conflicting signals about what goals to pursue and what was important. None of them supported a team-based structure. Could their problems be solved by just making changes in rewards and controls? Should they begin changing these systems now, or wait even longer to see what changes in strategy and structure would be made? Wasn't it time to just do it? Who should decide? Who should manage the implementation?

The point of this book is that there *are* appropriate answers to these questions. What is needed is a framework for organizing them—something that will help a manager use his or her own experience to make the choices that are appropriate for their organizations and their particular situations. Making these decisions in the context of radical changes in technology, competitiveness, and workforce values requires new logics for change. Understanding them is the beginning for real change.

All models of organization design have logics of *content, configuration,* and *change,* although they are rarely made explicit. Content refers to what is included under the heading of "organization design." It helps to answer the question of what can be changed to solve our problem. Configuration refers to how these elements of design are arranged with respect to one another. Are all of the levers for change equally important, or are some more important than others? The logic of change specifies the order in which the elements are transformed during implementation activities. Must we always begin a change process with strategy, or does it sometimes make sense to just change rewards? The three logics of content, configuration, and change help us answer the many important questions that arise in large-scale transformation activities.

The sections below compare and contrast three major stages of organizational evolution using these logics. These three major stages are bureaucratic (Stage I) forms, complex (Stage II) organizations, and adaptive organizations (Stage III). Adaptive organizations are shown to be a third, *new* stage of organization based upon radically new logics of content, configuration, and change. When these ideas are correctly implemented, they create what I call an *adaptive culture*. Adaptive organizations are the goals of *MegaChange*. The characteristics of these organizations and cultures will be discussed as the last topic of this chapter.

Stages of Organization: The Evolution of Adaptive Organizations

Adaptive organizations represent a third, new and distinct stage of organizational evolution that will partially replace earlier bureaucratic and complex forms of management. I will discuss the first two stages—bureaucratic and complex forms—briefly below. I will then discuss the third stage—adaptive organizations—in depth. I contrast each stage using the three *logics of content, configuration, and change*. These differences are summarized in Figure 2.1.

Stage I: Bureaucracy and Human Relations

Bureaucracy is the most widely utilized organizational form in the world. We have all marveled at its achievements and suffered its indignities. Perceptions of bureaucracy are full of value-laden inconsistencies; negative images of "red tape," burdensome paperwork, and political inefficiencies mingle with positive perceptions of the logic and rationality of the approach.

The German sociologist Max Weber introduced the term *bureaucracy* while studying a research problem concerning the impact of large organizations on family structure.[1] To solve his problem he

Figure 2.1
The Three Logics of Change

EVOLUTION	LOGIC OF CONTENT	LOGIC OF CONFIGURATION	LOGIC OF CHANGE
STAGE I BUREAUCRACY	STRATEGY Not Emphasized STRUCTURE Hierarchically Complex SYSTEMS Linear O Focus WORKFORCE Dehumanized		Top Down Minimal Involvement Bureaucratic, Administration Implementation
STAGE II COMPLEX ORGANIZATIONS	STRATEGY Quantitative STRUCTURE Laterally Complex SYSTEMS Bifurcated Conflicting, O focus WORKFORCE Limitations of Performance		Top Down Greater Involvement of Consultants, Staff Mixture of Planned and Incremental Change Management as Separate Activities
STAGE III ADAPTIVE ORGANIZATIONS	STRATEGY Visionary, Human STRUCTURE Simpler in Context SYSTEMS Work/Family Integration WORKFORCE Capabilities Efficacy		Top Down, Bottom Up Greater Involvement of Doers Engaged Sequence on Non-Political Contribution

HUMAN REL'S WF PARTICIPATIVE

then

QWL ADAPTIVE

3 1

needed to abstract the characteristics of the large organizations, or "bureaus," that he saw replacing small farms and shops as the dominant employer of workers. This abstraction was the first statement of the properties of the bureaucratic form. However, to say that bureaucracy was Weber's creation would be wrong, both practically and theoretically. Practically, he was simply observing and writing about the creations of others. Theoretically, bureaucracy developed from many perspectives, especially those of early management writers like Fayol[2] and Urwick.[3]

Bureaucracy's *logic of content* was dominantly one of hierarchical structures, specialization of labor, and depersonalizing systems. The result was the functional form of organization. Regardless of how well intentioned this was (for example, to make selection and promotion more fair), it ultimately resulted in dehumanization. Think about your last interaction with a large bureaucracy. What was it like? Usually you interact with someone over a counter, and often through a small window. The purpose of the counter and the window is to separate you from the bureaucracy. Having a physical and social distance put between you and the operators of the bureaucracy depersonalizes you. When you have a problem you get to bend over and peer through a little window cut into a sheet of opaque glass and try to deal with your problems by speaking to someone that you can't really see. It is no surprise that this often causes resentment and anger in the people who are trying to use the services of the bureaucratic organization.

Many organizations are trying to change this fact and *re*-personalize themselves. So far it has been a slow process. While I was on sabbatical at Stanford and Berkeley, I needed a bank account in San Francisco. I opened one at a large, nationally known bank, but it soon became hard for me to see why they were still in business. When I wanted to make a transaction I waited in a line. If I wanted to know my balance while I was making a withdrawal I was directed to an electronic information center. This meant getting out of line and then getting back in if I needed anything else. When I asked a question about mortgage rates I was sent to another person. The final straw was when I attempted to make a deposit in my account and had to wait for an approval. I knew that sometimes an approval was needed for a withdrawal, but I had never had to have anyone approve a deposit before! The bank had so many boundaries, rules, and depersonalizing procedures that it was almost impossible to deal with them.

Banks, government agencies, and other large bureaucracies are attempting to change these negative features of an overly bureaucratized organization. The Postal Service is now selling neckties and stamps with cartoon characters on them. They are a perfect example of a failure to achieve *MegaChange*. Ties and cartoons do not hide the one-way mirrors and observation posts for checking on and monitoring workers who are presumed to be dishonest, disaffected, and lazy. What they fail to understand is that these workers are not that way naturally. They are being taught by their organizations that they are expected to behave that way.

Bureaucracy also places very little emphasis on strategy due to its origins in sociology. Structurally, it emphasizes hierarchy, rules, and procedures as the dominant means of coordination. The *logic of configuration* gave primacy to structure and systems as the primary ways of achieving organizational objectives of efficiency and rationality.

The *logic of change* was top down. The top manager was the organization designer. Few people outside the upper echelons of the firm were involved in designing new structures or systems. When I began my career at the Wharton School, one of the first large-scale changes that I participated in was the reorganization of a large government agency. When I asked how the new structure—one involving literally thousands of employees—had been designed, the answer was that it had been sketched out by the director of the agency on a napkin in the executive dining room. It was up to the rest of us to make it work! Change was unilateral, peremptory, and "by decree" in most instances. Change was infrequent in relatively stable business environments.

Bureaucratic firms flourished in an era of abundant resources, relatively stable technology, and moderate competition. The hierarchy made all important decisions. As technology accelerated and competition intensified, these structures were unable to compete. The same hierarchies that were extremely efficient for handling simple, clear, and repetitive tasks became overloaded when nonroutine situations arose. Human issues also limited the efficiency of overrationalized and depersonalized organizations. Numerous industrial experiments indicated that organizational performance could be hurt by adopting views of workers that were too simplistic.

Managers sought to find ways around these problems. One way attempted to humanize the work by allowing workers a chance to meet their "social" needs. This was the beginning of the "human relations" movement. The human relations efforts emphasized the social aspects of work and stimulated broad new interest in managing groups and teamwork. It emphasized humanizing the content of work, but the dominant motivation of organizations for adopting these methods was productivity improvement.

The second related innovation was to begin to move toward new, more complex forms of organization. These forms utilized lateral teams in combination with existing hierarchy to add more management "horsepower" to the firm. We now had more than one choice of organization (bureaucracy or complex forms), and so "contingency" views of organization design emerged.[4] These said that there is no such thing as the one "best" organization. Bureaucracy was best for simple routine tasks, and more complex forms were appropriate when competitive demands required higher levels of information processing and decision making. More and more organizations

adopted these complex forms of management as business environments changed.

Stage II: Complex Organizations and Participative Management

The three logics of content, configuration, and change were different for complex organizations. Changes in structure were the most important at this stage and cut across all three logics. Whereas Stage I bureaucratic forms emphasized structural "principles of management" that were believed to be true in all cases, Stage II organizations achieved significant improvements in productivity by explicitly violating these very same principles! Bureaucratic organizations emphasized ideas like "unity of command," "authority should equal responsibility," and "management by exception." These principles failed in difficult competitive situations. New complex structures like matrix organizations explicitly violated these principles. In matrix organizations workers had two, three, or even more bosses! Managers were held accountable, but did not have authority to direct the activities of those performing functions for which they were responsible. Dual chains of command—one for projects or programs and another for functions—made it difficult to know who should take the lead when things didn't go according to plan. *However, these new forms significantly outperformed traditional organizations in challenging industries like aerospace.*[5,6] Firms in other industries seeking similar levels of high performance soon adopted them.

The old Stage I principles assumed human limitations and protected workers from situations that were viewed as too demanding (for example, two bosses, unclear authority). When these principles were violated by the new Stage II forms, attention focused again on the assumed limitations of the workers that the principles had been created to deal with in the first place. But now there was a new and more difficult problem. Since violating the principles was necessary to get desired levels of productivity, we could not protect the workers from the very problems that bureaucracy had been designed to avoid.

Workers now had to deal with ambiguity and conflict for the structure to succeed. Human issues that had been "designed away" in bureaucracy had to be dealt with actively and directly. The task of finding the "one best worker" for the job had to be broadened to allow for the many psychological characteristics that became important when protective principles of management were violated. The content of personnel selection, appraisal, and training systems changed and began to emphasize characteristics like motivation, ability to work in groups, and tolerance for stress. Psychological considerations became more important than the physiological factors emphasized in the past. There was more human content in systems design at this point, *but it still dominantly reflected assumptions of human limitations rather than capabilities.* Stage I organizations designed away the influence of human limitations, while Stage II organizations coped with them. Both ignored human capability as a potential starting point for organizing and as a source of competitive advantage and revenue growth.

Strategy also played a bigger role in this stage of organization. Contingency views raised the question, "If it all depends, what do choices of organization depend upon?" One answer was strategy. Planning systems evolved from simple "extrapolative planning systems" (what we do next year will be what we did this year times some factor) to "business strategy,"[7] in which strategies were determined contingent on aspects of the competitive situation. The logic of content for Stage II organizations included strategy, but its dominant focus was on structural complexity and the psychological limitations of workers.

In Stage II, "everything depends on everything else" models of organization design developed in response to the overly simple strategy-structure-control thinking of Stage I. This logic of configuration was a significant advance over Stage I thinking, but it introduced problems of its own. The new models had to be situationally applied. Any element of design—strategy, structure, rewards, people, or tasks—could be the starting point for change. The most elegant and successful of these was Galbraith's "Star" model, which has contributed immensely to management practice. Most of the other models of complex organizations are merely alternative portrayals of Galbraith's ideas.

With so much choice, management "fads" began to be a problem with Stage II organizations. For strategy it was things like the "BCG matrix," for systems, "MBO" and "Sensitivity Training," and for structure, "Matrix Management." Throughout all of this, structural complexity dominated the logic of configuration and was the key driver of organizational change activities.

Stage II organizations required a different logic of change. In Stage I, top managers implemented change by decree. However, understanding these new complex forms of organization was much more challenging. Their workings were often tedious and arcane. New systems had to be invented to make them work, and these were often as complex as the structures they served. Change management became a professional discipline that was practiced within the organization by staff and from the outside by consultants. General managers and line personnel were less and less involved in managing change, leaving these tasks to "experts." Stage II organizations resulted in less ownership of key strategic and organizational decisions by the line management of the firm. This was good for consultants and bad for organizations.

Stage II organizations increased performance by adding new lateral channels of decision making that violated traditional principles of organization design. These newer complex forms of organization are necessary to manage changes in competition, technology, and values. Bureaucratic organizations cannot address these challenges. But the real issue is *how much* complexity is needed. Most organizations have made their systems and structures far too complex. As we discovered that increasing levels of complexity could produce improvements in performance, we overused them.

However, we cannot afford to solve all of our problems with more and more management. The values imperative prevents this. At some point complex systems obstruct rather than enhance performance. Higher productivity can require *less* management and *more* leadership. In the future there will be a better balance of complexity, leadership, and empowerment for achieving productivity goals.

Stage III: Adaptive Organizations

Stage I established the principles of management. Stage II achieved higher levels of performance by explicitly violating them. Stage III reinvents the principles of management in response to the forces discussed in Chapter 1. Stage II organizations were able to handle changes in competition and technology that Stage I organizations could not cope with. However, they were not able to respond to the values imperative due to their fundamental, but partially hidden, assumption of human limitations. Stage III organizations begin with the capability assumption. Consequently, they meet demands for increases in productivity and also satisfy new expectations regarding meaningful work, satisfaction, empowerment, work/family issues, personal development, and careers. These two sets of pressures—value changes and the need for "hyper"-productivity—are less conflicting than they seem to be on the surface. It is not an issue of achieving productivity while making sure that employees are appeased. It is really an issue of productivity through people.

There may be no other way to do it. Productivity and involvement are not antithetical. Meaningful work means effecting something. Productivity is a key aspect of personal satisfaction. Radical gains in organizational productivity necessitate high levels of workforce involvement. Organizations that give people a chance to be part of something, that encourage people to develop themselves, and that reward people for what they do achieve these levels of productivity. However, implementing these ideas requires new logics of content, configuration, and change based on human capabilities rather than limitations. Together, these make up the *new logic of adaptive organizations.*

Three New Logics for Adaptive Organizations
The New Logic of Content

The *new logic of content* requires that concepts of strategy, structure, and systems be broadened to include a greater emphasis on human values, goals, capabilities, and efficacy. This logic follows directly from the capability assumption and the discussion above. If we assume human capability rather than limitations, the content of organization design must change.

Individuals expect meaning from work, and contribute to organizations when they have opportunities for realizing that meaning. Dehumanized strategies, structures, and systems preclude and disparage opportunities for meaningful contribution. Organizations that utilize them cannot hope for the necessary high levels of workforce involvement and commitment. Stage I and II organizations did precisely that. Bureaucracy dehumanized the workforce, and complex forms stifled engagement with excessive structure and controls. Strategy became an end in itself, profits came before people, and making money became more important than making products. A balance sheet summarizes accomplishment, but it does not equate to it.

The new logic of content requires that concepts of strategy, structure, systems, and the workforce be explicitly broadened to contain more meaningful content. Human beings are not intrinsically motivated by earnings per share, but by vision, purpose, and accomplishment. They can be controlled by structures that overmanage them, but they cannot be empowered by them. Being at work is not the same as being engaged in it.

The New Logic of Configuration

This idea specifies a new relationship among strategy, structure, and systems that gives priority to supporting workforce engagement and capability. In this configuration the workforce is at the center of strategies, structures, and systems that facilitate, enable, and engage individuals in achieving the collective purposes of the organization. The workforce "centers" the model shown in Figure 1.1.

Stage II models of organization design and change emphasize the fit among model components.[8] Although fit is critical, there is no priority among design elements. Structure depends on strategy, but strategy depends on structure. Systems must fit with both, but they also influence both strategy and structure.

Stage III models broaden the definition of who is responsible for creating fit. The new perspective argues that the total workforce—managers *and* workers—creates strategies, structures, and systems to accomplish meaningful tasks that are beyond any single individual's grasp. Co-design by the entire workforce achieves radical gains in productivity and satisfaction. The workforce "owns" the strategy, structure, and systems and uses them to achieve its *collective* goals. It is the creator and architect of organizations and not just another element of design. It therefore takes a place at the center of the Stage III design model.

Older models were management-driven models. Who determined fit? Managers, consultants, and staff did. In Stage III *everyone* is involved in making these decisions. Managers and staff play a key role, but so do individual contributors. The workforce includes both of these groups. Radical gains in productivity require everyone's engagement. No one can be excluded. Not one idea can be lost. Different components of the workforce play different roles in this process, especially in the early stages of change, but participation in organizational decision making must be radically higher for everyone. The new logic of configuration therefore places the workforce at the center of the configuration of organization design elements.

The New Logic of Change

This new logic contradicts the old top-down model of strategy implementation that was dominant in Stage I organizations and even persisted through Stage II. The top-down view was virtually synonymous with the assumption of a simple, linear, strategy-structure-control implementation sequence. The old concept is too limiting for several reasons. First, although organizations *do* adjust their structures to facilitate strategy implementation, they also design their structures to obtain flexibility regarding the "unknowns and unknowables"[9] that are always encountered in strategy implementation. The link between strategy and structure is therefore *intentionally* imperfect.

Second, for all existing organizations, strategic-planning activities take place in the context of current structures. This fact makes the strategy-structure-control paradigm too simplistic at best, since in this case *structure would precede rather than follow strategy.* Finally, in the old paradigm the workforce plays little role in the design of change. Top managers set strategy, and workers blindly and obediently implement its directives. This is more consistent with "limited rationality" assumptions than the idea of "capable engagement," and it fails to recognize that everyone's contributions are necessary to be effective in today's environment.

The *MegaChange* model asserts that people seek meaning in work through accomplishment and contribution to shared organizational goals. They do not have to be ordered, manipulated, or tricked into contributing. Political barriers to participation, involvement, and contribution have to be removed. We need to rely upon open and direct change processes that involve the whole organization in designing, implementing, and managing for the future. Such a process must involve all of the workforce at the earliest possible stage.

At this stage we confront a paradox. Top-down models of change are clearly too simplistic and do not involve the workforce in designing the future of the organization. One alternative would be to attempt a bottom-up or grassroots change effort. However, research is very clear on this point: there are few or no examples of successful bottom-up change efforts. So we have a dilemma. Workforce involvement is essential but insufficient. Top-down change oversimplifies the change process and constrains involvement.

The new logic of change specifies a top-down–bottom-up sequence of development activities. What this essentially involves is coordinating two parallel implementation efforts simultaneously. The first effort focuses on strategy-driven, organization-wide changes in systems and structures. It is what most of us think of as *transition* management or strategy implementation. The second process produces a *transformation* in the organization's fundamental culture and beliefs. Both processes—transition and transformation—must work hand in hand to achieve successful, fundamental change. Transitions follow the normal logic of strategy-structure-systems, while the transformation process begins with the workforce for the reasons discussed above, as part of the new logic of configuration.

Following this new logic allows people (management *and* the workforce) to work with what they are most expert with. Managers engage strategy at the overall organizational level. The workforce engages the systems that directly impact their work. As transitions work from *strategy to structure and systems,* transformations work from *systems to structures and strategies.* With proper orchestration, the changes reinforce each other in a synergistic way. We do not want to transform the organization into a form that is not strategically viable (transformation without transition). Nor can we rely forever on existing capabilities, cultural assumptions, and values (transition without transformation). Both processes must work together to co-design adaptive organizations. The chapter sequence in Segment II of this book is organized to follow the actual sequence of top-down–bottom-up change. The final chapter expands on these discussions and illustrates the overall relationship of transition and transformational activities for achieving *MegaChange.*

Adaptive Cultures

When strategies, structures, and systems are designed using the new logics presented above, the result is what I call an *adaptive culture.* In this section I will summarize the major features of these cultures. A culture is a consistent, shared set of values, norms, and beliefs about how the organization should collectively conduct itself.[10] A culture exists in the minds of the workforce and permeates every aspect of organizational functioning. It is not merely descriptive; it is also normative. It says how things should be, even as we struggle to get there. It is idealistic, but not unrealistic. It is a destination for change.

There is an emerging consensus about what this destination is. In fact, it is remarkable how widely shared this consensus is. We are beginning to know, with greater and greater clarity, where we are going and what we need in management. The consensus extends across organizations and across manufacturing, service, and government sectors of our economy.

The dimensions of adaptive cultures presented below are derived from field studies of organizations attempting to obtain radical gains in productivity and satisfaction. These studies were performed in existing organizations. They were not start-ups or new ventures.

The dimensions presented below are explicitly *not* based upon existing standardized measures of organizational culture. A list of these pro forma characteristics can be found in any introductory textbook in management. The reason I avoid these measures is simple. Most of them have a research history that anchors them firmly in Stage I or Stage II organizations. I am more interested in the culture of Stage III firms—the organizations of the future. The dimensions are not likely to be the same, for the reasons advanced in Chapter 1 and in the first portion of this chapter.

The dimensions that I have derived also utilize managerial language and avoid psychological terms that render them less meaningful in everyday contexts. Their primary purpose is in stimulating organizational change and learning. The dimensions are derived from data obtained from manufacturing, service, and government organizations. They summarize input from individuals at all career stages and from many different functions. The dimensions were first obtained from analyses within firms and then tested across organizations. The results are remarkably consistent.

Dimensions of Adaptive Cultures

At one level a culture is a set of shared norms, values, and beliefs. At another, it has consequences for our behavior, both as individuals and when we cooperate with one another in groups. Adaptive cultures specify new ways of thinking, acting, and cooperating.

The Thinking Dimensions

There are three new ways of thinking that characterize adaptive cultures.

1. **External focus: constantly using your impact on others as the rule for evaluating and prioritizing your efforts.** The concept is similar to, but broader than, customer focus. Customer focus is

often used to refer not only to customers in the traditional sense of the word but also to other groups within the organization that require your outputs as their inputs, to employee groups, and so on. These uses of the word "customer" use the word as if it were not a word.

External focus is chosen to indicate that everyone concentrates on delivering critical outputs and services to groups and organizations that are outside their segment of the organization. Some are within the organization but external to the work group or team; others, like regulatory groups, suppliers, partners, or customers, are outside of the formal organization itself.

2. **Process-centered: understanding your role in implementing a business process, and making it your primary goal to serve that process.** This is also different from the thinking that dominated the 1980s. In Stage I and II organizations, *goals* were much more important than processes. In adaptive cultures, processes become much more critical. However, goals are *not less important* than in the past; processes are just *more important.* Actively managing and improving processes is a key element of the new culture. Serving adjacent elements of the process is what the first dimension—external focus—was all about.

3. **Ownership: individuals taking responsibility for organizational outcomes, rather than organizations taking responsibility for individual outcomes.** In Stage I and Stage II organizations, managers took responsibility for individuals' performance. Authority flowed down the organization, but responsibility flowed up. It was management's job to plan, coordinate, direct, and control the activities of their subordinates. In adaptive cultures, individuals assume ownership of responsibility for the performance of the collective organization. "It's our job" replaces "It's not *my* job." This dimension is synergistic with serving

4 5

external groups that you are linked to in a common business process. Ownership means taking responsibility for their success as well as your own.

The Acting Dimensions

There are two new ways of acting in adaptive cultures:

4. **Speed: using agility, quickness, and responsiveness as an expected standard of behavior, and as a substitute for extensive analysis.** "Just do it" replaces "paralysis by analysis," and organizations learn by doing and acting. In hypercompetitive environments, there is little precedent to guide us. Effective organizations discover the future by acting quickly and learning from their experience. Analyses are outdated by the time they are completed. Speed means acting quickly in the context of process understanding and the needs of customers, suppliers, and partners.

5. **Initiative: originating your own actions, and not waiting for someone else to be the stimulus for your activities.** It means constantly seeking out opportunities for organizational improvement rather than responding to requests from others.

The Cooperating Dimensions

There are three new ways of cooperating in adaptive cultures:

6. **Collaboration: treating everyone as a partner and colleague, and working together to solve problems.** It means optimizing joint outcomes rather than individual ones. Collaboration is more than teamwork, because it takes place outside of as well as within teams. Functional work groups are not teams, but they can behave collaboratively.

7. **Nonpolitical: making decisions based upon characteristics of the problem, as opposed to political characteristics of the context.** This is very different from much of what is practiced

and taught today. Incremental change approaches use politics and manipulation as their primary tool for implementing change. We have learned that such changes are not sustainable. Business schools model and teach political behavior, rather than showing how to avoid it. Too much energy is spent on tactics of manipulation and personal gain, and too little on constructive problem solving.

8. **Boundaryless: performing your job and meeting the expectations of others without respect to the constraints of your formal organizational position.** Boundaries in organizations are not all bad. They group people who are most interdependent and actually facilitate their cooperation. They permit the development of specialized expertise. However, they also create identifications that inhibit cooperation. People define themselves as a "marketing" person, or as part of "production."

Crossing these psychological lines is far more difficult than would be imagined. Boundaryless means cooperation across these artificial divisions without giving up the benefits that they were created to achieve. The boundaries can be internal or external to the organization. We need specialist knowledge coupled with a generalist orientation. Boundaryless is very closely related to the initiative, process-centered, and external focus dimensions.

Summary

Chapter 1 introduced adaptive organizations and summarized the forces that require them. In this chapter I discussed where these ideas come from and how they are related to earlier thinking about organization design. Adaptive organizations are a new third stage in organizational evolution that will partially replace bureaucratic and complex forms.

Adaptive organizations are based on three new logics of organization design. These logics of *content, configuration,* and *change* require humanizing strategy, structure, and systems; placing the workforce at the center of the model of organization; and managing change as a top-down–bottom-up process. These are major changes for both theory and practice.

The research evidence concerning the effectiveness of firms utilizing aspects of this model is a source of both comfort and concern. On the one hand, the benefits of participation, involvement, and empowerment are overwhelming. Systematic and carefully done research indicates that performance gains of 50 to 60 percent are possible and even probable when these methods are implemented.[11] There is cause for great optimism at both the individual and organizational levels.

Yet all is not well. Despite these results, few organizations have adopted these new work methods. Virtually none have completed the development process that is presented in this book. Despite the logical appeal and demonstrated benefits to productivity and the quality of work life, most organizations continue to manage in the "old way."

I believe that this must change in response to the forces discussed in Chapter 1. We have asked workers to change but have done little ourselves. We are trying to implement new organizational forms using the old logics. We cannot create participative organizations without participation, and we can't break down boundaries by maintaining them between management and workers during the change process. Outside consultants reduce our ability to achieve cultural objectives like ownership when we allow them to substitute their initiative for ours. Political stakes in existing arrangements prevent new forms from emerging. Who must design adaptive organizations? The answer is clear—the organizations themselves. This will require using the new logics of change and not the old ones.

This ends Segment I of the book. Segment II—*MegaChange*— follows a chapter sequence corresponding to the steps in the top-down–bottom-up change model presented above. Each succeeding chapter presents the major transformation activity that must be accomplished at a critical stage of the overall change process. Each chapter also presents the concepts, actions, and tools that are appropriate at that step. These concepts, actions, and tools are then illustrated in the context of a major transformation process as described in the introduction to this book. We will apply the ideas of *MegaChange* to Lucent, Citicorp and Price Waterhouse. At each stage of change, using these tools will ensure that the major issues essential to moving on to the next level have been met. Segment III of the book—"Achieving Cultural Change"—discusses the overall integration, fine-tuning, and institutionalization of adaptive organizations.

MegaChange

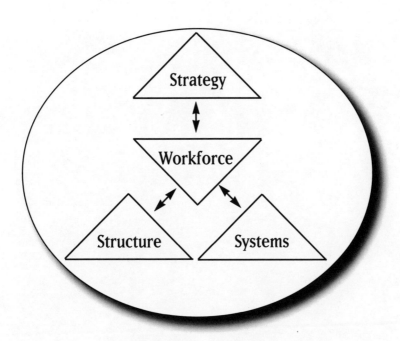

CHAPTER 3

Empowering the Workforce

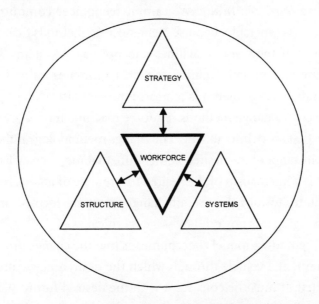

In this portion of the book we turn to a systematic discussion of each of the four major components of the *MegaChange* model. Chapter 2 described how the content of these components and the configuration among them are different from earlier models of organization design. The new logic also specified a change process that was both top down and bottom up. The first stage of this process focuses on *empowering the workforce.*

The Method-As-Model Principle

This chapter introduces two major change concepts. The first is the "method-as-model" principle. This concept asserts that the methods that are used to change organizations must themselves model the desired future organization state. This concept is especially important in the early stages of change. People become skeptical very quickly when they are asked to participate in a change process whose fundamental nature and form are not consistent with the stated objectives of the change. For example, it is not possible to successfully debureaucratize *bureaucratically!* We cannot reengineer commitment, integrity, and ownership, because reengineering methods treat organizations as if they were machines and not social systems. Every change method models, reinforces, and legitimates an end state. Bureaucratic change methods reinforce bureaucratic change goals. Reengineering change methods reinforce machine models of organizations that are dehumanizing. The change methodology is the first concrete instance of the desired new culture that members will experience. It is a microcosm of the desired future state of affairs. Important attitudes toward the overall change effort are formed on this basis. Managing this powerful message is critical.

The method-as-model concept means that the change process is the fundamental vehicle through which the desired new culture is transmitted. It must be consistent with the desired future state, in *form* as well as intentions. If not, we will be sending the wrong message—one that can totally undermine the objectives of the change. Large corporations frequently engage prestigious consulting companies to implement change for them. They send a dysfunctional message to every one of their employees: change is not our job; we can pay someone else to do it for us. It is not surprising that many such organizations fail to improve, despite the competence of the consulting firms that they have hired. This also happens when internal staff units are assigned primary responsibility for change; it becomes a staff activity divorced from the realities of the operating business. Such efforts are seldom taken seriously; they become the "program du jour."

Consider these examples of the fundamental inconsistency between intentions and method in most major approaches to organizational change. *Re-engineering*[1] talks about empowerment, but finds it very difficult to achieve using a framework that assumes that organizations are machines and that people are interchangeable parts. *Planned change*[2] methodologies fail to produce cultural change because they assume that top managers are omniscient and that workers are incapable of contribution. They fail when good ideas from the workforce come into conflict with the directives of top management and are ignored and legitimate participation and contribution are trivialized. *Incremental*[3] approaches view organizations as political systems and use political methodologies to change them. We are surprised when these methods inculcate precisely the same political characteristics that they are based upon, when political actions overwhelm productive activities, and when the organizations fail to get better. *Total quality efforts*[4] create quality "bureaucracies" that unintentionally divert the focus away from the very process improvements that they were created to implement. They crush initiative beneath tons of paperwork, meetings, and documentation. Over and over again we see examples of attempts to change organizations using methods that are fundamentally inconsistent with what we are trying to achieve.

Each experience of the change process is a model of what we are collectively trying to achieve. Individuals learn to understand and influence the future through these experiences and, as a consequence, to be comfortable with it. Behaving in the new way leads to thinking and feeling in the new way. Properly done, this produces the *adaptive culture* described in Chapter 2.

The following sections present the actions that must be taken, consistent with this rule, in order to begin empowering the workforce. Unfortunately, many firms' first steps in change are missteps. In fact, the early stages are often handled so poorly that they ensure that the organization will never progress to higher levels in the change process. This chapter presents the ideas necessary to avoid this failure.

Managing in the Early Stages: Creating Awareness and Legitimation

Many change efforts falter in the early stages, almost before they have begun. The first actions in empowering the workforce are management-driven and management-dependent. Essentially, they demonstrate management commitment. Without this commitment there is little point in proceeding any further.

There are five key actions that show top-management commitment. They are the following:

1. **Embrace workforce empowerment in the strategy and mission statements:** There are at least two types of errors possible here. The first is to embark on a major effort to involve the workforce but fail to have this effort represented in the strategy and mission statements. Most employees are very suspect of these statements in the first place. In this instance, failure to reflect the change initiative in the strategy says at least one of two undesirable things: the strategy statement is meaningless (as many may have already suspected), or the change effort is not important enough to be included in the strategy and therefore should not be taken seriously.

   The second critical error here is to announce the change effort as a critical element of strategy and then do nothing to support it. This is essentially the opposite of the first error and has the same consequences. It is necessary to make the change effort a key strategic initiative. The official strategy and mission statements should prominently include the goals of change initiatives. It is then necessary to support these statements with further commitment, as follows.

2. **Provide necessary financial support.** One of the quickest ways to sabotage a change effort is to not provide the resources necessary

to make the change succeed. Kurt Lewin,[5] the founder of the Institute for Social Research, discovered one of the most important ideas in change management. He observed that performance levels initially declined during organizational change. Actually, this should be expected as people learn new jobs, take on new responsibilities, and establish new work relationships. The objective of change management is to minimize these short-term costs and maximize long-term gains in satisfaction and productivity. However, there *is* a cost to change. Underfunding change activities minimizes short-term expenditures, but it also ensures that long-term gains will never be obtained. There are significant costs associated with adopting new work methods and new forms of organization. Organizations committing to transformation should be aware that radical improvements in productivity are not free. However, the costs of not making these investments far outweigh these expenditures in the current environment. Organizations can scarcely afford not to make these investments.

3. **Constantly provide the rationale for change.** "Why change?" is the question that must be answered, and appealing to the need to respond to competitive threats is not a sufficient response. The values imperative is being experienced by everyone today. It is necessary to understand that productivity must be obtained *simultaneously* with higher levels of satisfaction and quality of work life. These two goals must be understood as complementary and joint. Achieving them simultaneously achieves higher levels of performance, as discussed in Chapter 1. Workforce issues are *not* being accommodated solely as a means to higher productivity. Empowering the workforce ensures radical, sustained, and proactive productivity—*competitive advantage*—through meaningful work. Meeting this higher standard ensures that current productivity

issues are addressed while pursuing even more challenging objectives, as I discussed in Chapter 1.

4. **Support flexible implementation.** This is an early example of the method-as-model concept. The methods used to change the organization must model the desired change, as noted above. In the early stages of change, this means that management must allow latitude for local adaptations of the change effort. What works in one unit of a large corporation may be somewhat different than what works in another. A unilaterally imposed change *program* is inconsistent with involving the workforce in a change *process* that they help shape and tailor to their culture and business needs. A process of codetermining the design of change directly models and reinforces the desired outcome of greater workforce engagement.

5. **Display emotion for the change concept.** The actions above address key implementation issues concerning the objectives, logic, and support of the change effort. This action requires management to become directly involved in the change on a personal level. There are two aspects of this. The first is behavioral, and follows from the modeling idea in the preceding paragraph. If we want to operate in a new way, then management has to behave in this new way. When we do not live up to the goals of the change effort, we are sending a very powerful signal that we intend the change for others and not for us.

I have asserted that management frequently asks others to change but fails to change itself. When this happens, managerial behavior explicitly undermines the desired changes. However, it is not easy to change. Sometimes when top managers behave in the "old way" it is because they are having difficulty changing their own behavior. This is problematic because others may misinterpret this as a lack of support for the change.

It is therefore absolutely critical that management displays a constant emotional involvement in the implementation effort. If we cannot change our behavior immediately, we can show that we unequivocally support the change and are doing our best to adopt it. That we are not there yet does not detract from the validity of the effort. Real change is hard. Emotional support indicates a commitment to achieving it.

A Performance Model for Empowering the Workforce

The preceding sections have specified the necessary management actions in the early stages of change. The actual process of empowering the workforce begins after these steps are under way. The first actions were primarily management-driven. The next steps focus on developing a mechanism for workforce-driven change that will complement the managerial actions already taken and those to be taken in the future.

The change mechanism or "tool" for empowering the workforce that is presented below is based on a fundamental model of human performance in organizations.[6] This model is the second major concept of this chapter. The model proposes that work performance is a function of three critical factors—motivation, ability, and job understanding—as shown in the equation that follows:

Performance = Motivation x Ability x Understanding

This simple equation is very powerful. It says that three key factors determine work performance. The first is the individual's *motivation* to perform the task. People will be motivated to perform in a particular way if the performance leads to things that are valued.[7] These rewards may be things like money or a promotion, but may also include important intrinsic outcomes like autonomy, responsibility, and an opportunity to achieve something meaningful. These internal rewards can actually be even more powerful motivators when used appropriately.

However, motivation alone is not enough to ensure effective job performance. Individuals must be *able* to perform the job. Often, in attempts to empower the worker, people are asked to perform in new ways, perhaps more democratically, or by becoming members of teams as opposed to individual contributors. Although they may be motivated to do this, and may genuinely desire to operate in the new way, they may not be able to function effectively until they acquire the skills necessary for functioning in this new environment.

Motivation and ability are not enough to ensure productivity if the workers do not *understand* their role in the organization, and capable people can spend enormous amounts of time doing the wrong things. Work understanding means appreciating the requirements of one's position in the organization. In new, less bureaucratic, Stage III organizations, achieving this understanding is more difficult. Normal aids like job descriptions don't make sense in boundaryless cultures that emphasize learning by doing, speed, and flexibility. Since organizations have not acted this way in the past, it is more problematic for people to understand what effectiveness means in adaptive organizations.

The performance model means that all three factors—motivation, ability, and understanding—must be present for effective work performance. If any element is missing, the multiplicative nature of the model says that nothing will happen. This well-established research finding has very important implications. It requires a change mechanism that explicitly creates each of these three factors. Many efforts fail because the tools they use do not account for *any* of the three factors. The following sections present the critical actions that must be taken to stimulate motivation, create ability, and develop understanding. They follow directly from the method-as-model and performance concepts presented above. The final section integrates these criteria in the form of a tool for accomplishing these objectives: Action-based workshops.

Motivation: Awakening the Need for Involvement

The first component of the performance model is motivation. Executives frequently complain that "People just don't want to change!" or "People don't really want to be involved." For the most part, when this is observed it is due to poor implementation and a failure to understand the principles set forth in this book. It has been believed that the appropriate way to involve people in change is to ask them if they want to participate in our "program." Given that many organizations have created so many programs that have failed, we should not be surprised when the response is negative. No intelligent person wants to spend hours and hours of time in useless activity, in which their interests are only being accommodated as a means of achieving goals desired by others, and in which there are so many meaningless interventions under way that it is impossible to see how they are all supposed to fit together. Situations like this are more common than most of us would like to admit.

On the first day of one of my recent consulting engagements, I asked my client to tell me what activities they had under way that were similar to what they had engaged me to help them with. There were over 18 such initiatives that were currently going on! Taking any of them seriously is problematic in a situation like that. We should not be surprised to get a "NO!" from people asked to participate in such a silly undertaking. Unfortunately, this leads many managers to misunderstand the true potential and critical role of the workforce in creating radical change.

The proper way to motivate workforce engagement in the change process requires understanding of some sophisticated aspects of motivation theory. Some people like to say, "Theory is where the rubber meets the sky!" I like the quote and sympathize with it. But all management research is not bad or irrelevant. Unfortunately, without understanding some important points in motivation theory, practice falters.

How does someone become motivated to contribute to reshaping and reforming the corporation? The answer is not by asking them to participate. You must involve them directly. You do not tell people they are empowered, you empower them. This action bias flows directly from a little-understood and paradoxical finding in motivation theory.

Probably everyone who is reading this book has studied or heard of Maslow's "hierarchy of needs."[8] It is one of the most taught topics in all of management theory. It is in every basic management textbook. It is widely discussed in executive programs. It is also almost completely wrong!

Maslow's theory says that people have a set of basic needs, that these are arranged in a hierarchy (some are more important than others at different times), and that in order to motivate someone we must appeal to the need that is active at that point in time. A large volume of research based on the model has clearly shown that the needs contained in the model are not the basic categories of human needs, and that these needs are not arranged in the hierarchy portrayed by the model. In other words, the model is almost completely wrong.

Despite this, the model continues to be taught. In this way, it shares some similarities with older models of change like the Planned Change model, or even with newer concepts like Reengineering. It doesn't seem to matter if something is right, as long as it is appealing.

But here is the paradox and the subtle point that I alluded to above. When people have attempted to implement the Maslow model they have frequently obtained positive results! How can a model that is almost completely wrong yield positive results in application? Answering this question tells us how to motivate workforce engagement in the early stages of the top-down–bottom-up model of change.

One of the most important attempts to improve on Maslow's hierarchy was made by Clay Alderfer[9] of Yale University. He proposed that we could understand which needs were driving behavior by utilizing a few simple rules. One of these rules was that the more a need is satisfied, the less important it becomes to the person. There are many familiar examples of this. Most of them are physiological. For example, the more food you eat, the less interested in food you become. Alderfer believed that when higher-order needs like "social" or "achievement" needs became satisfied, they would become less important.

When Alderfer tested his theory, he found out something quite interesting. For higher-order needs, the more they were satisfied, the more they became important! This explains the paradoxical findings on the use of Maslow's hierarchy. Even though Maslow's theory was wrong, most of the needs were fairly desirable. When programs were put in place to satisfy them, the programs actually *stimulated* the need in the first place. If we had asked workers to participate in such programs, they would have said (and often did say) no. But once they were in them, they became very involved and avid supporters of the changes. The conclusion is clear: It is not enough to ask people to be involved or to tell them they are empowered. We must involve, engage, and empower everyone directly or nothing will happen.

If all of this seems a little abstract, here is a case illustration of what I am talking about. It is from the consulting experience of my friend Robert Guest, one of the pioneers of the job enrichment movement. Bob had been helping a division of Ford Motor Company implement an "Employee Involvement" program. Employee Involvement teams had been set up and workers had been invited to participate. One older, tough, first-line supervisor named Red had been invited to attend meetings but had refused repeatedly. Finally, after being told that he would not have to work at the meetings, that there would be refreshments, and that some of his friends would be there, he agreed to go, but not to contribute.

Red steadfastly lived up to his commitment not to participate, but after a few sessions things began to turn to topics in which he was interested. You could see that he wanted to talk, but was holding back. Finally, one day the topic of a high scrap rate on one of the machines in Red's area came up. The problem was generating huge costs and no one could understand why it was occurring. Finally, Red spoke up and said: "If you want to know why that machine is throwing off so much scrap I'll tell you. About three years ago, one of those new industrial engineers came down here and changed the lubricant on that machine in order to save a few cents a gallon in cost. The day the lubricant was changed the machine started to throw off scrap. If you want it to stop, change the lubricant." The lubricant was changed, the scrap stopped, and Ford saved about $3 million per year.

When Red was asked why he hadn't said anything about this before, he said, "Because no one ever asked me." This wasn't true, but Red thought it was. He had been asked before. What he really meant was that he had really never been involved before. He had been asked but not engaged. Again, it is not enough to ask people to be involved, or to tell them they are empowered. We must involve, engage, and empower everyone directly or nothing will happen. This mistake is made over and over again, and will continue to repeat itself until the point is recognized. If we want people to be motivated to be involved, involve them. The result will follow, and the workforce will take responsibility for its own contributions.

Ability: Enabling Action

Motivation, as noted above, is not enough to ensure performance. People must also be able to perform in the new way. Empowering the workforce requires making some "enabling" changes in systems to accomplish this purpose. *MegaChange* means behaving in new ways. Although these changes are consistent with natural tendencies toward accomplishment, satisfaction, and self-determination, Stage I and II

organizations have taught people not to expect these opportunities in organizations. On the basis of wrong assumptions, they have unintentionally created strategies, structures, and systems that explicitly suppress them. As a consequence, changing to this more natural way of working is more *unnatural* than we would expect.

It is therefore important to help enable the change by devoting resources to developing the abilities that older forms of organization suppress. It is foolish to ask someone to behave in a team-oriented way when they have never worked on a team. It is hard to behave in a "boundaryless" way when you have lived in an environment of rigid job descriptions that explicitly forbade such behavior. How is one to know how to behave toward an old supervisor who is now a "team facilitator"? Behaving differently requires support that facilitates and enables it.

In the early stages of change, this essentially means that we must provide training that leads rather than lags the change. The old top-down change model said, first change strategy, then change structure, and then train people in their new work roles. The new logic of change is top-down–bottom-up. We must enable people to be an active part of the change process itself. This means that training must lead rather than lag the change. It is hard for people to contribute when they have been taught how not to. We must actively work to change the sequence of training activities.

The second thing that must happen is that line managers and workers should perform the training. This is a direct consequence of the method-as-model concept. Change (and training) is everyone's responsibility. Localizing these first steps in the Human Resources function teaches people to believe that they are not personally responsible for helping others to learn new skills and develop neglected abilities. Alternatively, co-learning from peers and line managers models the desired new culture. Learning from the Human Resources staff separates learning from action, and ultimately efficacy from productivity. Learning at an off-site meeting is less powerful than learning from the people that you work with in the context of your own job. Although training is the traditional province of Human Resource professionals, *their* human resources are insufficient to accomplish the large-scale training necessary for real transformation. They will also have significant new challenges in other areas (large-scale systems changes) as the process develops.

There will be two main consequences of these changes in the training process. First, the training may not be as elegant as it has been in the past. Teaching is a skill, just like managing or operating a machine. If someone has never done it before, it is likely that some of the teaching materials may be a little rough, that someone might provide an example that is not perfect, or that the speaker may be a little nervous. That is what change is about—doing things differently. If we were trying to just do what others had done a thousand times before, there would be no rough spots. There would also be no learning and little gain in competitive advantage. The rough spots are a small price to pay for greater relevance and immediate application in the job.

The second consequence is that individuals begin to learn that they are responsible, not only for their own learning and skills, but also for the learning and skills of others. These modest first steps model the key dimensions of the adaptive culture. They are critical because they set the tone for what will follow. Small mistakes here generate big costs and even failure later on.

Understanding: Acting in the New Way

Motivation and ability are not enough to ensure performance. Individuals must also understand what acting in the new way means. Capable, motivated people can spend enormous amounts of time doing the wrong things. It is easy to misunderstand how to behave in the new culture, for the same reasons that training in new skills is required. Stage I and II organizations have taught people how to

behave in dysfunctional ways. They have taught us what not to do rather than what to do. When these older forms of organization become obsolete, we are left without models of how to perform. Many misunderstandings result. Some people believe that being empowered means doing anything they want, and they do! Understanding is required to help people know what is expected in the new culture. Training develops the abilities necessary to do the new things well.

The primary way that people learn to understand their roles in any change is by doing. Changes in competition and technology, coupled with the values imperative, create an environment that is so volatile that older analytical methods (like job descriptions) are obsolete by the time that they are created. The method-as-model concept is directly relevant. If the culture described in Chapter 2 emphasizes *speed* (dimension 4) and learning by doing, than learning to understand new roles should be done in this way as well. A change method that models the new culture will be more effective.

Learning by doing basically involves three related activities. The top-down–bottom-up model means that managers and the workforce have complementary roles in this process. In the early stages it is managers that *demonstrate* the desired new behaviors. Workers observe these acts and attempt them themselves. They then *practice* them and *refine* them. Demonstrating, practicing, and refining are the three key activities in learning by doing.

The process is not as one-way as it may sound. Managers are also attempting to act in the new way as they understand it. But their understanding is imperfect. Although they may be modeling a new way of working, they are practicing their roles just as much as the workers are practicing theirs. They refine their understanding of what managing in the new culture means based upon feedback from the workforce. This co-learning process is the behavioral complement to the training process discussed above. It models almost every key dimension of the adaptive culture.

The sections above provide a specific set of criteria for creating change. The process must conform to the top-down–bottom-up model that is the new logic of change. This means that the first steps in empowering the workforce are management-driven, as described in the early sections of this chapter. Following these, specific actions must be taken to begin workforce-driven change. The performance model requires that these actions produce motivation, ability, and understanding. Both the management-driven and workforce-driven aspects of empowering the workforce must strictly adhere to the method-as-model principle. If any of these conditions are not met, nothing will happen.

The next section presents a tool called the action-based workshop that has been specifically designed to meet these criteria. It is a tool for achieving higher levels of productivity and culture change simultaneously. Used correctly and in conjunction with the management-driven actions discussed above, it completes the process of empowering the workforce.

Action-Based Workshops: A Tool for *MegaChange*

The ideas presented above are very important for understanding the basic principles underlying the first critical step in *MegaChange*, empowering the workforce. Without this understanding, organizations attempting large-scale change are doomed to mimicry and dependence on outsiders for innovating their own organizations. I believe that it is time for institutions to take responsibility for their own futures, and this means understanding how to change and reform them. This is not a task that should be left to others.

It is very useful to have a tool to implement the ideas presented above. The preceding discussion has emphasized a set of concepts for guiding change activities. Specific actions were developed for implementing these concepts. A tool incorporates the concepts and actions developed above into a specific integrated mechanism. I call the tool for empowering the workforce an "action-based workshop." It is directly based on the action recommendations above. I emphasize learning by doing instead of by analysis. We should teach, rather than hire teachers. We must involve people in change rather than merely communicating it to them. Action-based workshops integrate these specific practices into a cohesive mechanism that implements the top-down–bottom-up, method-as-model, and performance model concepts.

The name "action-based workshop" also derives from a critical idea in psychology—the idea that attitudes follow actions. This idea is similar to the motivational ideas presented above, but more extensive. The importance of this idea cannot be overestimated. We are attempting to create the culture described in Chapter 2. This culture has three core aspects—what I have called the thinking, acting, and cooperating dimensions. How can we change how people think about their work and their relationships within the organization? The answer lies in the fact that attitudes follow actions. When people act differently, they begin to think differently. This guides behavior in the future and further reinforces change. Action-based workshops involve everyone in behaving differently. Attitudes supporting these new behaviors—a key part of cultural change—result naturally from this process. The method not only models the new culture, it actually produces it.

The management-driven change actions discussed under "Managing in the Early Stages" should be initiated before the first action-based workshops are begun. Following this, there are three key activities in implementing action-based workshops: (1) managing attendance at workshops, (2) implementing the workshops themselves, and (3) managing follow-up. Each of these will be discussed below.

Managing Attendance: Targeting the Workforce

The first decision in implementing action-based workshops is deciding who should attend. The answer is simple: participation should be extensive, even to the point of being exhaustive when possible. Everyone is not relevant to all problems, but everyone *is* relevant to the new adaptive culture. Ideally, everyone who will be involved in the new organization should participate. The whole idea of *MegaChange* is that radical improvements in performance and satisfaction (the higher performance standard from Chapter 1) can be achieved only if we base our organizations on human capabilities rather than limitations. It would be foolish to organize based on capabilities and then not use them!

We must also be absolutely sure that we meet the method-as-model criteria. This also requires that as many people as possible be involved because we do not want to model the idea that transformation can be accomplished by consultants, internal bureaucracies, a small group of managerial "insiders," or "professional" volunteers for change programs. As discussed above, this is precisely the reason that many Total Quality and Reengineering efforts fail. The method must model the need for broad ownership of the change process. Demonstrating otherwise stops the effort before it even has a chance to begin.

Everyone should participate for these reasons. However, everyone cannot attend at the same time. The process of involving people in action-based workshops therefore has to be managed. Figure 3.1 helps us to make the decision of who should attend. It shows that there are four categories of interest in participation in a workshop, based upon the degree of influence that people hold in the organization.

At the center of the diagram are people who are already empowered. In the early stages of change these tend to be managers and political insiders. Some of these people deserve to be empowered and others do not. The next ring signifies the set of people who are currently not empowered but who would like to be. Often these people are middle managers and staff people. Moving outward to the next ring are people who could be empowered and engaged but who are not aware that this is the case. Red, the Ford employee from my discussion above, is a good example of someone who would fit in this category. Finally, there are people who truly do not want to participate or be involved. They are happy to perform their work fairly and energetically, but do not want to exercise discretion about how it is performed. They want to accept direction from others.

There are two key points to be made from this simple diagram. First, the number of people in the outer ring is far smaller than is normally imagined. Managers frequently ask me, "What about the people who do not want to be involved?" They mistakenly *overestimate* the number of individuals in the outer ring of Figure 3.1. This happens because most managers do not implement the performance model as discussed above.

When we simply tell the workforce they are involved rather than actually empowering them, people who can be productively involved are not stimulated. Like Red before the involvement meetings, they continue to misunderstand their own motivation to contribute and choose not to participate. Managers observe this behavior and reach the wrong conclusion—that these workers cannot be involved. As a consequence they confuse people in the outer two rings of Figure 3.1. That is, they confuse people who *could* be productively engaged in change with those who *cannot*. By concluding that the former group is really a part of this latter category, they seriously overestimate the size of the group that truly does not want to be involved in self-determination. Having gained this false understanding and believing that the workforce does not want to be involved, managers then fail to model the power-sharing behaviors that they must demonstrate to the workforce to produce understanding—the third component of the performance model. The result is a vicious cycle of disengagement that prevents change from happening almost before it has begun.

Figure 3.1 makes a second point. There are some individuals and groups in organizations that need to be "de-powered." This conclusion follows directly from the *nonpolitical* and *ownership* dimensions of the adaptive culture (dimensions 3 and 7 in Chapter 2). Many

Figure 3.1
Targeting the Workforce

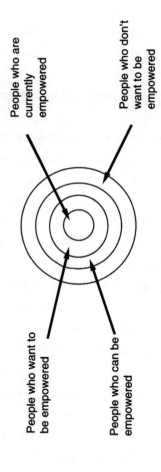

People who are
currently
empowered

People who don't
want to be
empowered

People who want to
be empowered

People who can be
empowered

Some people need to be "de-powered":
Useless staffs
Checkers checking checkers
Politicians

Work from second circle out in initiating change:
Early success
Spread commitment
Test boundaries
Depower, empower

Number who can be productively empowered is larger than normally presumed.

organizations have large, useless staffs. With little meaningful work to do, these groups attempt to create work for themselves. They do this by politically taking over some of the useful work that needs to be performed. However, when they do this they move the work from where it should be to where it shouldn't be—that is, away from the people who have the most knowledge to perform it. Ownership becomes piracy, and incompetence replaces efficacy. There is hardly anything worse than a political staff unit with little to do.

Everyone can think of a useless staff unit. But we have to be careful to distinguish between units that are useless "by design" and those that are merely poorly implemented. This subtle point can be seen very clearly in the case of most Human Resource groups.

There is probably no staff function as important today as the Human Resources function. It is a vital, necessary part of creating future success. But how do most organizations staff these units? With people who have training outside the Human Resources area. Most of them have good interpersonal skills —they get along well with others. But most of these people do not have the critical skills necessary to manage the Human Resources function for the future. Human Resource personnel need to be good at strategy and organization design, not just at hiring and benefits. The changes in organizations that are sweeping the world are posing new and very sophisticated challenges that require specialized competence in Human Resources. Yet we populate these critical groups with precisely the people who do not have this competence. It is not the Human Resources functions that are at fault here. It is the line managers who have implemented them who have failed.

Other staff units are, however, useless "by design." The famous organization theorist Victor Thompson[10] proposed a simple rule for detecting this problem. Can you attach a reasonable and identifiable body of knowledge to this staff? If not, it is *useless by design*. You have created a staff unit that has nothing to do by definition. If there is an identifiable body of knowledge but it is not being delivered, then we have a staff that is *useless in implementation*. We want to de-power those who are useless by design and empower those who are useless in implementation.

The final group that needs to be de-powered are the politicians. Politicians put personal gain above the gain of their colleagues and the organization. Sometimes they have learned that such behavior is appropriate from change methodologies that use political methods to manipulate and trick people into contributing. Some politics is inevitable in organizations, but too much politics is devastating.

Generally, the process for empowering the workforce through action-based workshops moves from the inner rings of Figure 3.1 outward. This respects individuals' desires to be involved, generates success, and spreads commitment. Once broad participation has been gained, political agendas begin to fall. Some will try to cling to obvious political positions in the face of rational evidence of their inappropriateness. The workshop process must ensure that ownership of critical change issues does not become concentrated in the hands of the wrong people. A process to accomplish this follows.

Organizing an Action-Based Workshop

There are four components of an action-based workshop, as shown in Figure 3.2. These critical activities are *informing, identifying, working,* and *responding*. Each of these is discussed below, along with some answers to frequently asked questions about implementation of this important tool for *MegaChange*.

Step One: Informing the Workshop

The first activity at an action-based workshop is a step called *informing*. This step follows directly from the top-down–bottom-up logic. Informing is necessary to make sure that whatever is accomplished at the workshop is consistent with business purposes. Action-based workshops are focused workshops. They are focused on achieving higher levels of productivity, satisfaction, and engagement—the higher standard of performance discussed in Chapter 1. They must not be allowed to stray from this purpose.

Informing is generally management-driven. The first step in an action-based workshop is therefore usually led by the top manager of the business. At later stages, as workshops spread, it becomes the manager or team that has responsibility for the business unit, project, program, or process that is the topic of the workshop. Generally, action-based workshops begin with self-contained business units and then spread downward in the organization. The early sessions are more general, and later sessions focus on specific business issues and processes.

At the beginning of the workshop managers inform the group about two main things. They should first present the business issues confronting the organization and the firm's strategy for addressing them. Following this, they should discuss the goals of the change effort of which the workshops are a part. These two activities are an opportunity to reiterate the actions described in the first part of this chapter under the heading "Managing in the Early Stages." An effective informing session communicates the strategy and the goals of the change effort. It must also clearly signal the importance of workforce involvement, financial support, the rationale for change, and the need for flexible implementation and display a clear and unwavering emotional support for change. If this cannot be done, the workshops will fail.

This process generally takes from one to two hours to complete, although some managers can productively use more time. It ends with the leader issuing a challenge to the group that will be the focus of the remaining time in the workshop. The challenge is normally a business challenge that requires everyone's engagement for resolu-

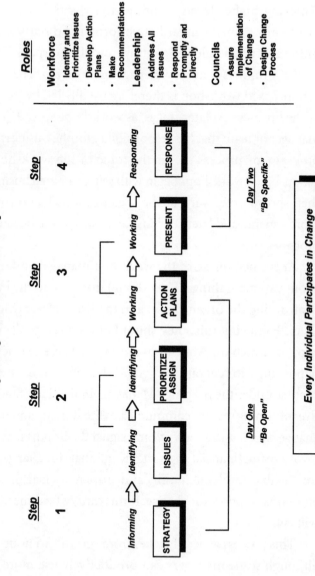

Figure 3.2
Organizing Action-Based Workshops

Roles

Workforce
- Identify and Prioritize Issues
- Develop Action Plans
- Make Recommendations

Leadership
- Address All Issues
- Respond Promptly and Directly

Councils
- Assure Implementation of Change
- Design Change Process

Step 1 — Informing

Step 2 — Identifying

Step 3 — Working

Step 4 — Responding

STRATEGY → ISSUES → PRIORITIZE ASSIGN → ACTION PLANS → PRESENT → RESPONSE

Day One "Be Open"

Day Two "Be Specific"

Every Individual Participates in Change

tion. The process for addressing it, that is, the action-based workshop, is the actual mechanism for achieving cultural change. Taking action in the context of the workshop *models* the desired new culture while achieving real gains in productivity, workforce involvement, and satisfaction. The process is both transitional (to new levels of performance) and transformational (to a new culture and set of values). The next stage of the process is using the large group to identify specific issues that must be resolved to address the business challenge issued in the informing stage.

Step Two: Identifying the Issues

This step *identifies* the specific issues that will be the subject of action planning in the next stage of the process. There are two key activities in the identification step. They are generating and selecting issues.

There are a number of ways to *generate* issues. One way is to interview appropriate people before the meeting and then present the results of the interviews to the large workshop group. A second, preferred way is to use a "nominal group"[11] methodology with the entire workshop group to generate the issues in "real time." In this process, each person nominates the idea that they believe would be most effective in addressing the challenge issued in the informing step. Each person contributes only one idea at a time, and no one may critique the ideas until later. Each person is asked to contribute individually, and each has a turn in the process. Every idea is recorded for the selecting step that takes place next.

The nominal group methodology is attractive for a number of reasons. First, it is very active. People are not just responding to a set of ideas from interviews. They are creating the ideas in the first place. Second, it is difficult to not be involved. Each person is called on in turn. People may "pass," but they are still directly involved in the process. Frequently, people who have never been involved before pass on their first time through the process but then enter the conversation shortly thereafter. This process directly engages people in the third ring of the "targeting" model shown in Figure 3.1. Third, the nominal group method avoids anonymity. People are associated with the ideas that they raise. This models the ownership dimension of the adaptive culture. People must not believe that when they raise an idea it is an issue for someone else to resolve. The process is a high-energy, high-involvement event. It is a legitimate chance for people to be heard in ways that they have never been before.

Selecting from these ideas can also be accomplished in many ways. It is important because the group must narrow down the issues that it will address. The nominal group technique discussed above will typically generate between 50 and 80 ideas. There are too many to work on in a single workshop, so they must be narrowed down. One good way to accomplish this is multi-voting. In this process, each person receives a specific number of "votes" that they can cast for the ideas that they would most like the group to focus on. Multi-voting follows the idea generation process. The issues receiving the most votes become the topics for the next step in the process—working.

Step Three: Working the Issues

In this stage, groups *work on* specific sets of issues identified in the preceding step. Each group develops action plans that will be presented as the last step in the workshop. Groups should be composed of from five to nine members. Above that number, the groups begin to act like little "organizations" and become less effective for problem solving.

A frequently made error at this stage is to attempt to "facilitate" the problem-solving activities within these groups. It is true that many of the people in these groups may be relatively inexperienced in teamwork and in problem-solving methodologies. Facilitation is tempting in order to overcome these barriers. However, facilitation places the productivity goals of the workshop ahead of the cultural change objectives. It is critical that the workshop model ownership, initiative, boundarylessness, and the other characteristics of the adaptive culture. It is this culture that will produce sustained high levels of productivity, and not the other way around!

Facilitators teach dependence on others for solutions, separate the process of problem solving from the problem, and substitute staff assistance for line involvement. They reinforce that idea that accomplishing things that are natural and fundamental requires special assistance. The basic human need and tendency for cooperation is treated as if it is something unnatural that has to be facilitated by experts rather than allowed to proceed. For the most part, experience suggests that facilitated groups rarely produce more effective action plans than nonfacilitated groups, and that they obstruct cultural change objectives in the process.

Step Four: Responding to the Action Plans

In this step, the groups formed in the preceding stage present their recommended action plans to management. Again, this combination models the top-down–bottom-up change logic. Although the workforce is presenting to management, both co-determine the course of action and share the responsibility for producing it.

Usually, the presentations are made to the top manager of the business or business unit that is the home for the issue being addressed. In some cases, the "top manager" is really a team of people who are jointly responsible for the business process being studied. In either case, it is their responsibility to address the plan being put forward and to support it appropriately.

This can be a difficult step in the workshop for management. Many of the ideas that are put forward challenge past practices, and all of them call for change. Some may be openly critical of decisions that have been made. There may be legitimate disagreements about how to proceed. It is management's job to *respond* to every issue that is raised, but not to implement every one of them! An effective action-based workshop is not a "love-in." Neither is it an opportunity for management to dispose of every idea that people might advance for change.

Some of the ideas and plans will be good ones, and others will be less so. In the responding stage it is critical that everyone's ideas are heard and responded to, even it they are not ultimately put into action. It is even more important that good ideas are implemented and that change begins to happen as a direct consequence of the workshop activities. When this happens management accepts the team's recommendation (often with modifications made by other teams) and assigns responsibility for implementing the plan.

It is generally preferable to not assign responsibility for implementation to existing staff units and management exclusively. It is better to let the team that developed the action plan take responsibility for implementing it, with appropriate support. This directly links planning and doing and creates ownership. It also demonstrates that everyone is responsible for change, not just management and staff. This stage of the workshop concludes with a summary of the actions that have been agreed to, the specific responsibilities for executing the plans, and a timetable for their accomplishment.

Managing Follow-Up

Action-based workshops model the adaptive culture and directly address all elements of the performance model. Used correctly, they are a powerful tool for empowering the workforce. Unfortunately, successful workshops are not enough to accomplish this purpose. Something tangible must happen because of the experience. It is possible for people to leave a very productive action-based workshop still doubting whether anything "will really change."

Most workshops fail because of poor follow-up. Commitments are made and never consummated. Lack of follow-through teaches people that doing nothing is as acceptable as accomplishment and action. People learn that public pronouncements are equivalent to private renouncements.

An effective way to avoid this problem is to schedule a follow-up session at which teams present the results of their activities up to that point. The presentations are made, not only to management, but also to the other teams that were present at the original workshop. No one wants to be embarrassed by their lack of accomplishment, and follow-up to the commitments made at the workshop are usually vigorous. Some actions will have been accomplished, and others will still be under way. It is the sense of movement that is important. The most significant issues are often the most difficult to resolve, and we should not punish ourselves for making progress toward their resolution even if we cannot solve them immediately.

A "change council" should be created and assigned responsibility for orchestrating the action-based workshop process. This council should be composed of the top manager for the business, several members of his or her team, and representatives from various levels of the workforce. In addition, for large-scale change efforts (those involving over 500 people), it makes sense to dedicate someone to manage the council's activities on a full-time basis.

The council manages the workshop process and all the details associated with implementing it. The council assures follow-up and shares the results of change efforts within the organization. It is also their responsibility to capture "best practices" from the workshop, to avoid duplication of effort as the workshops multiply, and to continuously improve the process.

The Lucent GROWS Transformation— Empowering the Workforce

In this section I illustrate the concepts, actions, and tools described above in the context of a highly visible organization and a major cultural transformation effort—the Lucent GROWS transformation.

I appreciate the cooperation of Fred Lane and Craig Gill, of Lucent—key architects of the intervention—for making this information available and for involving me in the transformation.

Formation and an Immediate Challenge

Until 1996 Lucent Technologies was the communications equipment unit of AT&T. Until that time AT&T managed the businesses that would comprise Lucent through various divisions and subsidiaries. In April 1996, an IPO was completed, and on September 30, AT&T distributed all of its shares of Lucent to its shareholders.[12] At that time Lucent became independent of AT&T.

Since then Lucent has flourished. A share of Lucent at the time of the spin-off had tripled in value by the end of 1997. Profits soared 43 percent during the same period.[13] The company benefited from pent-up demand for equipment from local carriers and long distance carriers who were reluctant to order from AT&T and who until the formation of Lucent had been competitors in the services business. The creation of a separate company allowed Lucent to capitalize on this pent-up demand.[14]

In 1998, however, growth was forecast to slow. Lucent's big businesses are highly competitive, and AT&T—Lucent's biggest customer at 10 percent of revenues—was planning to cut $1 billion from capital spending in 1998. In response to these challenges Lucent realized—*despite the fact that it was a mere two years old*—that it needed to transform its culture.

Lucent GROWS

Despite these challenges, Lucent did not abandon its aggressive growth goals. In the 1997 annual report Henry Schacht and Richard McGinn, the chairman and the CEO of Lucent, reported that the company was "strong operationally, organizationally, and financially.

. . . We are poised for growth and for high-performance results that produce increased shareholder value. *That means reaching higher. And that's what we intend to do*" (emphasis mine).[15]

There were several key strategies that Schacht and McGinn intended to use to make this happen. Organizationally, the most important of these was the GROWS effort. Lucent had already began to focus on what it wanted to be other than "not AT&T." In addition to identifying the key strategies that were needed, they also began to ask what the cultural requirements were to reach their aggressive growth goals. Strategically, they knew that they wanted to be a "high-performance company" and built this into their strategy and mission. They said that they wanted to grow the top and bottom line in double digits year after year, and realized that the consistency in this earnings growth was critical. They were keenly aware of what had happened to Motorola when their earnings had faltered.

Initially, they could get this growth through improvements in operating efficiencies. But soon they realized that they would have to grow revenues as well. Like many organizations, they quickly found out that the cost reduction methods used by GE and others only worked for a while. Unlike most other organizations Lucent, with its strong heritage in innovation, realized that more of the same would not get them where they were determined to be.

They then began to systematically identify the cultural characteristics of "high performance companies." Five key dimensions of culture were identified and are shown in Table 3.1, along with the dimensions of the adaptive culture developed in Chapter 2. As can be seen, they are very similar and align almost perfectly.

There are a couple of important points about these cultural dimensions. First, they are strategically relevant for Lucent. Second, they represent some but not all of the dimensions of the adaptive culture. This is appropriate because each organization will have different strategic priorities. The five dimensions that Lucent chose to focus on are not the only dimensions of culture that matter. They are

Table 3.1
Lucent GROWS and the Adaptive Culture

	Thinking		Acting		Cooperating	
Adaptive Culture	External Focus	Process Focus	Ownership	Speed	Initiative	Collaboration	Non-Political	Boundaryless
Lucent GROWS	Obsessed with Customers and about Competitors			Speed	Global Growth Mindset	Workplace that is Open, Supportive, and Diverse	Results Focus	

the five dimensions *on which there was the greatest gap between where they were and where they strategically wanted to be.* Each organization should tailor their cultural change objectives to the areas where the most change is needed, using the adaptive culture dimensions as a guideline.

During the time that this bottom-up cultural work was being done, a simultaneous top-down change effort had begun to implement their emerging new strategies. Supporting these changes in strategy required a major reorganization. Lucent was therefore directly employing the top-down–bottom-up model of transformation discussed in the preceding chapter. They knew that they had to change the tires on the car while it was running! Cultural transformation— *MegaChange*—required that top-down transition activities had to occur simultaneously with bottom-up transformation activities.

Top management also supported the bottom-up process by ensuring that all of the criteria demonstrating top management commitment were met. The cultural change initiatives were included in Lucent's strategy and mission. Resources were provided both financially and organizationally. Fred Lane, a senior manager who had been with AT&T through the Lucent start-up, was assigned the job of managing the cultural transformation. The reasons for the change were constantly repeated in corporate communications. The method chosen to implement the change (described below) was designed to fit their situations.

Lucent realized that the real change that they wanted was between people's ears, and that a mechanism was needed to accelerate the cultural transformation. Working with outside consultants who had a deep familiarity with the organization, they developed an intervention strategy utilizing a variant of the action-based workshop model. These sessions were called JAM sessions—for Joint Action Method.

The JAM sessions clearly illustrated the method-as-model principle, and included all four of the major steps in the action-based workshop method: informing the group on strategy, identifying and working key issues, and, finally, having key business leaders respond to the ideas of the group. The meetings were cross-functional and cross-level, *modeling boundarylessness*. Ideas were identified and developed within the sessions and business leaders responded on the spot to all ideas, *modeling speed*. Individuals were given specific assignments based upon the recommendations of their teams, *modeling ownership*. In short, the method-as-model principle was explicitly applied in the development of the sessions.

The performance model was just as important. Individuals were involved in these efforts and not simply told they were "empowered." This produced *motivation*. Senior leaders demonstrated, practiced, and refined the new behaviors that the culture required, producing *understanding*. The approach paralleled the key components of the performance model advocated above. Motivation, ability, and under-standing combined to produce significant first steps in cultural change. Lucent had begun the *MegaChange* process.

Summary

This chapter has presented a set of concepts, actions, and tools for empowering the workforce and then illustrated these with reference to the Lucent GROWS process. Empowering the workforce is the first step in the process of *MegaChange*. Two critical concepts were introduced in this chapter. The first was called the method-as-model principle. This requires that whatever change mechanism and actions we utilize be consistent with the end state that we are attempting to achieve. The second concept was the performance model, which specified that performance is a function of motivation, ability, and under-standing.

These two concepts were used to suggest the actions or critical change factors that must be taken in empowering the workforce. The final sections of the chapter introduced a tool—action-based workshops—that integrates these concepts and actions into a cohesive mechanism for change. Collectively, these concepts, actions, and tools are both necessary and sufficient for accomplishing this first critical step in *MegaChange*.

The next step is *engaging systems*. As the workforce becomes empowered it quickly identifies local systems issues that impede rather than facilitate its performance. As more of these issues are addressed, larger systems problems that cut across the entire organization become apparent. It is to these systems issues that I turn in the next chapter.

CHAPTER 4

Engaging Systems

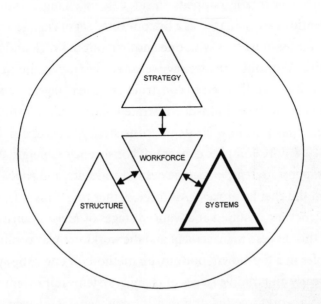

In this chapter I discuss the concepts, actions, and tools for *engaging systems*. Systems refers to organizational practices and procedures, operating processes, and human resource management tools. *Engaging systems* follows *empowering the workforce* because the workforce must play a critical role in redesigning organizational processes. The core concept of the chapter—knowledge-based empowerment—asserts that intelligent change requires us to utilize the expertise of those with the most knowledge of the processes being changed. Since the workforce operates most of the organization's systems, they must be actively involved in redesigning them. Engaging systems therefore follows the empowering stage of *MegaChange*.

The Critical Role of Consistency

At the engaging systems stage, our actions must not only build the new systems that are required, but do so in a way that continues to support change actions taken at earlier stages. This is quite different than what normally happens in large-scale change. Many large interventions are managed as a disconnected set of change activities, often at cross-purposes with one another, out of synch and noncumulative. Without consistency we often destroy at the next step what we so carefully tried to construct at earlier stages. We rely too exclusively on the old top-down strategy-structure-control model that emphasizes only strategic consistency. Successful change requires a more complex concept of consistency. Change activities must *support* strategy, *model* the desired end state, and *enable* earlier steps in the change process. All three, rather than only one, type of consistency are required at advanced stages of *MegaChange*.

In this process, management and the workforce play complementary roles in a top-down–bottom-up method for engaging systems. In the early and middle stages of change, systems improvements are primarily workforce (as opposed to management) driven. This is appropriate because the workforce has the most intimate knowledge of the systems that it uses to conduct its work on an everyday basis, and is in the best position to know how the systems need to be changed to improve performance. Management, systems design experts, and human resource specialists play a key role later in the process.

In order to explain this more fully it is necessary to introduce the core concept of this chapter. The concept is *knowledge-based empowerment.* Empowerment was explained in Chapter 3 using the performance model. Having said what empowerment is, we now need to distinguish it from the apparently similar concept of delegation. The concept of knowledge-based empowerment derives directly from this important distinction. Applying it indicates who should lead change at various stages of *MegaChange.*

Empowerment and Delegation

Empowerment is often confused with delegation. However, there are substantial differences between these concepts. Delegation is an old idea that was very important in Stage I organizations. The idea was to make sure that responsibility and authority were equal for every job. When delegation was implemented correctly, people had the authority that they needed to execute their responsibilities.

As practice moved to Stage II organizations, the concept began to run into problems. In complex organizations, responsibilities were confusing. People reported to more than one supervisor and had job responsibilities in more than one area. Membership on teams involved responsibilities to the team and to the functions that the team members came from. It was hard to know how much authority to delegate when responsibilities were unclear. People frequently found themselves in positions where they had substantially more responsibility than they had authority.

The concepts of responsibility and authority had to be changed. Stage I organizations emphasized the giving of authority by a managerial elite to a position at a lower level. Power was something management gave to the worker, within a closely determined zone of discretion. This idea led to the erroneous assumption that there was only so much power, and if I gave some of what I had to you, there was less for me to hold. This error led many managers to avoid sharing power at all costs. In Stage II organizations, the inconsistency between responsibility and authority created misunderstandings and made it difficult to be effective.[1]

In Stage III—adaptive organizations—responsibility and authority are reinvented and made consistent. Delegation is replaced by "empowerment," and responsibility by "ownership." These are not just differences in terminology. Authority and responsibility are *formal* aspects of organizing. They are based upon organizational properties and not individual capabilities, and they belong to formal roles in the organization. Empowerment and ownership are *social* aspects of organizing. They are based on individual efficacy and initiative, and not just on roles and requirements. They belong to people.

Empowering, therefore, means more than delegating. Assigning authority does not mean that someone has the ability, motivation, and understanding necessary to perform. Empowering them does. It is clear, therefore, that empowerment cannot take place without the knowledge that is necessary to create ability and understanding, and that the organization must allow this knowledge to be used.

Knowledge-Based Empowerment

Knowledge-based empowerment means utilizing individuals with the most knowledge of the problem for its solution. Unlike delegation, empowerment does not mean assigning someone to make a decision that you could make. It means enabling them to make a decision that, based upon their knowledge, they should make. Conversely, assigning people with little knowledge of the issues at stake is not empowering them; it is endangering them, for they will surely fail.

Application of this concept helps us understand the relative roles of management and the workforce in engaging systems. Who has the most knowledge of organizational systems, policies, and processes in the early stages of change? The answer is the people who live with them on a day-to-day basis, who operate within them, and who practice them—the workforce. Given the complexity of most organizations, management does not have enough actual day-to-day contact with the systems it has created to truly understand all of their implications and problems in application. This is not an issue of incompetence or neglect, it is a simple consequence of complexity. No one manager is smart enough to understand all of the systems that are necessary to operate a complex organization in detail. The workforce is in the best position to evaluate and change the systems they use to do their jobs. Using the knowledge-based empowerment concept means that the workforce should make systems decisions at early and middle stages of change.

In the latter stages of change this situation is reversed. In this case, novel new systems must be invented to help implement large-scale changes in strategies and structures. The design of these systems requires specialized knowledge of information systems and human resources. Experience suggests that the knowledge of these sophisticated systems design issues resides in the hands of specialists in these areas. Consequently, for large-scale systems changes that cut across multiple functions and require advanced technical understanding of specialized areas, management-driven change is appropriate. This ensures application of technical expertise, consistency across the organization, and the realization of economies of scale where possible. Knowledge-based empowerment means utilizing individuals with the most knowledge of the problem for its solution. Management and systems experts should make these decisions in the latter stages of change.

In the early and middle stages of change the knowledge-based empowerment concept means that systems changes should be workforce-driven. In the latter stages, application of the same concept means that large-scale, organization-wide systems changes should be management-driven. This division of labor reflects the expertise that both must bring to bear in achieving *MegaChange*. The following sections indicate the necessary actions and a set of tools for engaging systems in the early, middle, and latter stages of change that meet these criteria.

Engaging Systems in the
Early Stages of *MegaChange*

In the early stages of change engaging systems focuses on issues and policies that obstruct achievement and create dissatisfaction. As these are addressed, problems in *larger systems* are identified and resolved. These problems typically involve human resources systems, pertain to the larger organization, and cut across many areas of the company. Solutions are sought that apply to the whole organization.

Engaging systems is the first step in the critical process of changing not just the workforce, but also management. As a consequence, it is where many change efforts have stopped in the past. A large organization can spend up to one year just to reach this point. It is very important not to falter here. Many organizations have attempted employee involvement or empowerment efforts and failed at the engaging systems level. Some did not understand the concepts presented in the preceding chapter. Others managed to generate initial excitement and enthusiasm, but stalled when no real change in systems occurred. If further change is managed well, very significant improvements in productivity result, along with substantial progress toward implementing the adaptive culture.

Engaging Systems: Workforce-Driven Policy Changes

The first action-based workshops are learning experiences. Management is learning how to listen and respond, and the workforce is learning that their ideas are valued. Both are trying to understand their new roles in a more empowered work environment. Both management and the workforce are *demonstrating, practicing,* and *refining* new behaviors, as described in Chapter 3, and as a consequence are generating greater understanding of effectiveness in the adaptive culture.

Early action-based workshops have a very open agenda. Their primary objective is culture change, although there *is* also an immediate gain in productivity. It is important for participants in the workshops to understand that they are free to raise a broad range of issues and that there are no "taboo" topics. Executing the "informing" step of the workshop according to the guidelines from Chapter 3 ensures that groups will rarely get far off track.

Because an empowering format like the action-based workshop is unfamiliar, the topics that are raised in the "issue identification" step of the workshop tend to be concrete, more immediate, and clearer in early workshops. Participants' actions are tentative as they learn that taking the risk of speaking out is worth the reward of being responded to. Often issues that have been irritants for years can be resolved in hours. In the early stages, most of these issues tend to involve policies that are inappropriate. Resolving policy problems is the first step of engaging systems.

There seem to be three categories of policy problems. The first is simply bad policies. These are rules that never made sense in the first place. Examples would be things like too many signatures being required on expense reports, or having limits on equipment purchases that are so low that the cost of processing the paperwork exceeds the potential losses associated with raising the limits. Often these issues reflect Stage I and Stage II organizational thinking that was preoccupied with control through oversight rather that cultural control. *These policies need to be re-created and revised.*

The second category of policy problems contains policies that made sense before but that no longer fit the organization's current situation. These are "historical" rules, still on the books, and still creating a bureaucracy for their administration that persists despite their irrelevance. Meetings continue to be held to coordinate things that no longer need to be coordinated, and procedures manuals contain vast sections that pertain to procedures that are no longer practiced and will never be practiced again. *Historical and irrelevant policies need to be eliminated.*

A third category of problematic policies contains those that seem to be illogical or irrelevant but really are not. These are "maligned" policies. Often people will complain loudly about a particular practice or procedure with only a little knowledge of the policy. When they are given a chance to reframe it, they quickly come to the understanding that what seemed silly from a distance is really not so bad after all.

This can be quite functional as organizations learn why (for the first time) such a rule exists and why it is functional to maintain it. Experience suggests that problematic policies of the first and second kind are much more prevalent, but *when a maligned policy is encountered it is necessary to reinforce it and make its rationale clear.* Workshop participants and the council should do this. Management should not do this or it will risk appearing defensive.

The action-based workshop generates both culture change and productivity enhancement. Many early issues focus on minor "indignities" that people believe they have been enduring, and on ways of removing them. As things progress, concerns turn more toward issues of organizational productivity. Session topics begin to become more focused and thematic, less policy-driven and more concerned with systems than with isolated rules.

When this happens, the workshops encounter what I call the "discretion problem." How can a workshop that has only 50 or so participants design a system that may pertain to many thousands? How can we be sure that we have not reinvented the wheel? How can we know that what is being proposed will not harm rather than help the very system we are working on? It is essential that the action-based workshops create change. It is just as essential that this be positive change. Even though the process being followed emphasizes empowerment, there are still appropriate controls. Answering the discretion problem addresses the nature of these controls and shows how to achieve workforce-driven formal systems change.

Engaging Systems: Workforce-Driven Large Systems Change

The knowledge-based empowerment concept gives one answer to the discretion problem. In an action-based workshop, people are empowered to make decisions for which they have specific knowledge. That is the logic for letting the workforce engage systems change for practices that impact them directly in their everyday work environment. This means that the discretion problem is partly resolved at the selection stage of workshop design. We should not engage people in resolving issues about which they have little knowledge.

Even though we are producing high-quality, knowledgeable actions for engaging systems, the recommended changes may still need to be orchestrated. There are issues of consistency and efficiency to be considered. An intelligent change for one division may be less so for another. An effective global policy designed by one may harm the other. Every workshop should not address the same concerns. They should build upon one another. It is demoralizing to spend a lot of time resolving an issue that has already been resolved by someone else. It is not meaningful and thus does not advance us very far. These are issues that limit the discretion of the action-based workshop.

Empowerment therefore does not mean eliminating limits on decision making. It also does not mean unilaterally controlling them as in Stage I and II organizations. Addressing the discretion problem means guiding empowered decision making.

The tool for accomplishing this is the *change council*, discussed in Chapter 3. The council's charter is to orchestrate the action-based workshop process. Its specific responsibilities include tracking progress on implementation activities, discovering best practices, and coordinating change efforts.

These responsibilities address the remaining issues in the discretion problem. If members of the council are present in workshop sessions, they can easily point out when an issue has been addressed by another group and what the progress has been thus far. This avoids reinventing the wheel. The Council may also interject the learning from other efforts in the form of best practices that the group can build upon and refine. It may also carry issues that may have implications for the broader organization back to an appropriate management or staff group for further study (according to the knowledge-based empowerment principle, such a group would be the appropriate decision maker for this type of issue).

An Example: Work and Family Issues

One category of issues that usually need to be handled in this way are work and family concerns—one of the most important sets of issues in management today (as I pointed out in Chapter 1). Work and family issues are encountered almost immediately as action-based workshops move beyond their early stages. Will telecommuting be allowed? Will the company sponsor child care? What about "flex-time"? For baby boomers, what allowances will be made for people with elder-care responsibilities? Anyone who has dealt with these issues understands that they are difficult to resolve effectively. Many different positions are held concerning whether these practices are fair, appropriate, or even effective.

Frequently, decisions about what to do are assigned to the Human Resources staff, who recommend actions to senior management. Most senior managers are middle-aged and over, and they are predominantly male. Their closest exposure to conflicts between child care and work responsibilities is in discussions with their working children. They are too far removed from the values changes that we discussed in Chapter 1 to understand the real issues at stake, and as a consequence should not be the "deciders" in this instance.

However, coordination and specialized expertise are still needed. Management provides the coordination, and specialized staffs (usually the Human Resource function) add expertise. The stimulus for change and an understanding of the problem come from the workforce. The task is to utilize as many good ideas from the workforce as possible. Management must be made aware that there really is a problem.

The council is responsible for making sure that both of these objectives are met, as well as for handling questions about work/ family issues in the workshops. During a workshop, it would be the council's responsibility to make it clear when a work and family problem is an issue that is beyond the scope of any single workshop. But it would also be their responsibility, along with the workshop leader, to make it clear that these issues are important, that the group's input is essential, and that these concerns will be addressed.

Workshop participants provide input to the decision process by developing action plans for addressing work/family concerns. The council coordinates and aggregates these plans with those from other groups. They then present them to senior management for action. Staff groups help by developing detailed plans that respond to the workforce concerns and that incorporate as many of their ideas as possible. The result is a large-scale formal systems change that originated with the workforce.

The necessary actions and responsibilities for addressing the four issue types—bad, historical, maligned, and discretion problem issues—are summarized in Table 4.1. The next step in engaging systems addresses *processes*, a relatively neglected topic until recently. There is a great deal to be gained by more actively managing processes, from both the cultural change and productivity standpoints. Focusing on processes begins to develop the *thinking* dimensions of the adaptive culture while producing very significant gains in productivity and revenue enhancement. However, there is a right way and a wrong way to do it. The method-as-model and knowledge-based empowerment principles show that the right way is for process changes to be workforce-driven. This creates ownership and utilizes the expertise of those with the most intimate knowledge of processes—the workforce.

Table 4.1
Issue Types and Actions in Workforce-Driven Systems Change

Issue type	Actions	Responsibility
Bad policy	Reinvent the rules	Workshop teams before follow-up meeting (1 month)
Historical policy	Eliminate the procedures	Workshop teams in mid-term (3 months)
Maligned policy	Educate the workforce	Council
Discretion problem	Coordinate and implement "best practice"	Council with senior management and staff

Engaging Systems at the Middle Stages of Change
Taking on Major Processes

Organizations have only recently become interested in managing processes. The dominant thinking in management has been goal oriented rather than process focused. Managing goals effectively is a critical aspect of *MegaChange*. I will address it specifically in Chapter 6, "Remaking Strategy." Unfortunately, management's appropriate interest in managing goals has resulted in an unintended neglect of processes. Attention to both is necessary to achieve high levels of productivity and satisfaction.

In the old way of thinking, management and workers jointly negotiated their goals and the rewards to be received when these goals were attained. This method was intended to ensure that people were motivated to work toward goals that accommodated management's interests as well as their own. There was also a step in this process in which managers and workers developed a process through which the goals would be achieved.

Like many good ideas in management, these goal-setting ideas were often poorly implemented. One of the chief problems was that the process became bureaucratized and divorced from line management. It became a process that was run by staff, who, in order to ensure that they maintained control (and had something to do), developed elaborate techniques for goal setting and performance appraisal. When managers faced the burden of completing so much paperwork, most of which was irrelevant and unnecessary, they opted out of the process. The first thing to go was the process-planning stage. It was easier and quicker to set goals and agree on rewards. Bureaucracy killed the first attempts at process management, just as it is now killing TQM.

Under intense pressure from competition and technology, organizations have rediscovered processes. Coordination, cooperation, and responsiveness require process understanding, and organizations have been working aggressively to obtain it. Managing processes is perceived as something new, and as a consequence as something somewhat mysterious. In a rush to embrace these new ideas, many firms are erroneously neglecting goals, forgetting that, after all, goals are what processes are created to serve. Organizations are going outside of their own expertise to hire consultants that presumably can help them manage processes more effectively.

This approach is mistaken, for all the reasons that were advanced in Chapter 3 and above. Outside consultants do not and cannot afford to understand a firm's processes as well as can those that work with them on a daily basis. Hiring them teaches people that they are not responsible for what has to be one of the most central aspects of their jobs. Assigning processes to staff or consulting units creates boundaries where there should be none, decreases ownership, and puts people in a responsive rather than a proactive, initiative-seeking role. It is just wrong.

Process improvement efforts should be workforce-driven and management-guided. Management is in the best position to know what processes are needed. The workforce is in the best position to know how to modify, improve, and reinvent them. Process improvement should follow the top-down–bottom-up, method-as-model, and knowledge-based empowerment concepts closely.

Engaging Systems: The CitiGroup Team Challenge Effort

The CitiGroup Team Challenge effort provides a positive example of the concepts, actions, and tools for workforce-driven systems change. Team Challenge is a method for involving the workforce in a variety of organizational change initiatives. It produces improvements in organizational performance and simultaneously changes leadership behavior and organizational culture. It is therefore a tool for *MegaChange.*

Jim Noel, a vice president for executive development at CitiGroup at the time that Team Challenge was initiated, and David Dottlich describe the process as follows.[2] The early stages of Team Challenge focus on creating the necessary preconditions for change. Participants are selected and formed into teams to address an important business issue that will form the "challenge." These early steps taken at this stage correspond to the actions recommended in Chapter 3 for empowering the workforce and creating awareness and legitimation for change. Participants are selected on the basis of their ability and relevance to the challenge, and top management signals its commitment and support for the Team Challenge process and the importance of the business issue that they will work on.

Once participants have been selected and teams have been formed, they begin to work on the challenge that has been assigned to them. This could be improving an important business process, such as working across boundaries or developing future leaders. As Team Challenge moves forward, activities focus on team building and building understanding of the problem that the teams have been asked to address. After an initial workshop that launches the challenge, teams engage in data gathering that involves customers, best-practice companies, external experts, and senior management. With this data in hand, the teams develop action plans and present recommendations to senior management, detailing how these challenges should be addressed.

At the presentations, senior leadership has a chance to challenge the recommendations and to understand the analyses and data that support them. Shortly after this meeting, the leadership works with the group to decide on what specific recommendations will be pursued, and to assign responsibility for implementing these decisions. Those assigned responsibilities must report their progress back to management at a later point in time.

The general structure of Team Challenge corresponds to the major portions of the action-based workshop model, although it takes place over a longer period of time and uses a different methodology for identifying the problems to be addressed. This illustrates that different tools for change are possible. What is important is that the tools that are chosen are based on the concepts underlying the *MegaChange* model.

All tools must meet our criteria of supporting strategy, modeling the desired change, and enabling earlier steps in the process. At the *engaging systems* stage, the most important concept is the knowledge-based empowerment principle described above. This concept ensures that the actions taken will *support* strategy because those making the decisions will be the most knowledgeable about the strategic processes being changed. In order to *enable* earlier steps in the *MegaChange* process and *model* the desired culture, any tool that we use for engaging systems must also be consistent with the critical concepts from the *empowering the workforce* stage of the process. This means being consistent with the method-as-model principle and the performance model discussed in Chapter 3.

The CitiGroup Team challenge process passes these important tests. First of all, the participants are selected and the teams are formed so that their members will have relevant knowledge and a diversity of background that will bring new perspective to bear.

Where detailed knowledge of the issues at hand is not present, it is developed at the launch and data-gathering phases of the process. This satisfies the requirements of the knowledge-based empowerment principle.

Participants are put in a situation where they are being called upon to make important recommendations for change. They are not simply told that they are empowered, they are *actually* empowered. This fits the requirements for producing motivation in the performance model from Chapter 3. Since they were selected for Team Challenge on the basis of ability, thoroughly oriented to the nature of the team's tasks at the initial workshop stage, and develop relevant data, all of the ingredients for high performance are present. In Team Challenge, Performance = Motivation × Ability × Understanding, a clear example of the performance model.

Finally, Team challenge meets the method-as-model principle. Data gathering touches a number of sources inside and outside of the firm to gather data on key processes, modeling the external and process focus dimensions of the adaptive culture. Team members must take responsibility for presenting their recommendations and the reasoning behind them to senior leadership, modeling *ownership*. Teams are often cross-functional, requiring collaboration and boundaryless behavior. Finally, each member is encouraged to take individual initiative, and the recommendations of the teams are acted upon with speed. Team Challenge supports the firm's strategy, enables earlier stages of the *MegaChange* process, and models the adaptive culture.

Strategic Process Workshops

The CitiGroup Team Challenge process is a powerful tool for systems change. An alternative methodology uses strategic process workshops for this purpose. Strategic process workshops are modifications of the action-based workshops presented in the last chapter. They are specifically designed to focus on two of the thinking dimensions of the *MegaChange* culture, process and external focus, while continuing to build the acting and cooperating dimensions that were impacted in earlier stages of *MegaChange*. When strategic process workshops are used for large-scale systems change (usually following simpler AB workshops) all of the adaptive culture dimensions are impacted. Strategic process workshops therefore enable earlier stages in *MegaChange* while simultaneously modeling the desired culture and directly supporting strategy. They are a powerful tool for change.

There are four varieties of strategic process workshops. These vary in terms of their depth of intervention into organizational processes. All of them build upon the action-based workshop model and continue to reinforce the desired acting and cooperating aspects of the adaptive culture. They are the primary tools for implementing the thinking dimensions of the cultural change.

The four types of strategic process workshops, in increasing order of depth of intervention, are called "Focal Process," "Mapped Process," "Process Mapping," and "Critical Process Identification" workshops. Each of these, along with criteria for selecting among them, is discussed below.

Focal Process Workshops

Focal Process workshops are the first step in the evolution of the basic workshop model. They are essentially similar to the normal action-based model and do not deviate from it in most respects. The principal difference is in the issue that is addressed. As described above, early sessions focus on policies and large systems changes. In those cases, the focus of the meeting is determined by the issues raised by those in attendance. In the case of the Focal Process workshop the overall topic of the meeting is an organizational process selected by the change council in collaboration with management.

The topic of the meeting is announced in advance, and after selecting the particular process to be addressed, the remaining portions then become largely workforce-driven. Meeting the knowledge-based empowerment principle means that participants in the workshop must be very carefully selected to ensure that they have knowledge relevant to the specific, often cross-functional process being considered.

No "process mapping" activities are undertaken in this format. It should be selected when the focal process is well understood and there is little ambiguity about what the process is and what, specifically, it is intended to accomplish. Without this common understanding, there is little chance of a constructive dialogue among participants in the workshop. When the process is not clear, another variety of strategic process workshop must be used.

Process Mapping Workshops

The Process Mapping workshop is the next step in the evolution of strategic process workshops. It is appropriate when there is less understanding of the actual workings of a process, but broad agreement that it is important. In this case, work to clarify the process is justified.

The Process Mapping workshop engages participants in "mapping" the process *in the context of the workshop*. Other aspects of the action-based workshop process—identifying, working, and responding to issues—proceed normally following the process mapping stage. The addition of this stage is the major modification to the action-based workshop model.

Execution of this model requires that the group possess skills in process mapping. Some facilitation of the mapping process may be required. To reinforce the ownership dimension of the adaptive culture, this facilitation should not be done by consultants. It is more effective to have this performed by people who have been participants in earlier Process Mapping workshops.

This model presumes that the process being improved can be understood within the time constraints of a two-day meeting, and that the actual work involved in mapping the process will leave sufficient time to develop and respond to action plans for improving it. When this is not the case, and process confusion is more profound, the process must be mapped outside the workshop experience itself.

Mapped Process Workshops

In this variety of strategic process workshop, the process that will be addressed receives considerable study before the actual workshop begins. This prework by the group that will be leading the workshop represents an additional step in the action-based workshop model. Unlike the process mapping step that occurs *within* the Process Mapping workshop described above, *this step is accomplished before the meeting begins.* This is necessary to allow sufficient time to understand a process that would be too complex to address in a shorter time.

The Mapped Process workshop begins with a presentation of the work of the group that performed the pre-meeting analyses. Often the new process map will indicate significant problems that have been overlooked due to misunderstanding and ambiguity about just what was supposed to be happening. The mapping process is very illuminating.

Following presentation and discussion of the process by the workshop group, the steps of *identifying, working,* and *responding* to issues proceed based on this new process understanding. The results can be startling, and improvements generating huge cost savings are not uncommon. Equally important, the Process Focus dimension of the adaptive culture is becoming firmly established so that these improvements become institutionalized rather than isolated events.

The three types of strategic process workshops discussed so far have all presumed that there is agreement that the process being improved is a necessary process. When there is a lack of fundamental agreement about what the core processes necessary to operate the business are, the next level of workshop is necessary.

The Core Process Workshop

As we reach this stage of intervention into processes, the knowledge-based empowerment principle dictates that the workshops become more management-driven. Management has responsibility and a set of skills for managing the organization as a whole. It is therefore the most knowledgeable about the processes that are "core" to its overall functioning. However, the top-down–bottom-up change logic requires that decisions regarding these processes include as much relevant knowledge from the workforce as possible. The workforce's role evolves from mapping and suggesting improvements in processes that currently exist to anticipating and correcting problems with processes that are in the process of development. This is a far more challenging role.

The Core Process workshop model recognizes the challenge of intervening so deeply. As a consequence, it is more labor intensive than other models. Management begins the workshop with a presentation of a proposed set of processes and a broad outline of their major steps. These processes are normally derived from the strategic planning activities of the business (performed by line managers and *not* by consultants and staff). This step corresponds to the informing step of the action-based model, but is much more intensive.

Subsequent steps are similar to the action-based model, but are more difficult due to the amorphous nature of the proposed core processes. They are only partially defined, and have never been operated. Everyone's knowledge is incomplete. The workforce is asked to develop an implementation plan for key aspects of the process being studied. The plan is presented to the business leader. Rather than implementing the plan directly, its strengths and weaknesses are noted. The council accumulates the results of these discussions.

Since the groups are beginning with a very undefined process, identifying and refining promising core processes extends over several workshops. The promising outputs of the first workshop become inputs for the second. Since different people attend the second workshop, the potential core processes are given exposure to a wider set of people than existing processes receive in the models discussed above. Successive workshops propose, reject, and refine potential core processes until there is consensus about what they are and the plans for implementing them. This amount of work is extensive and is only justified in cases where a fundamental shift in core business processes is desired. Although this is costly, the method continues to model the critical cultural dimensions of initiative, ownership, collaboration, and process focus, while breaking down boundaries between management and the workforce. It therefore accomplishes radical change in processes while meeting the method-as-model principle.

These four types of strategic process workshops are illustrated in Figures 4.1–4.4, along with their major features. Table 4.2 summarizes the criteria for selecting among them, as discussed above. Selection from these models should follow the "minimum intervention" prin-

Table 4.2
Process-Mapping Methods Arrayed by
Depth of Process Intervention

Type	Depth of Intervention
Action-Based Workshop Process	Low, Process Assumed Known and Necessary
Process Mapping	Moderate, Process Assumed Knowable, Understandable within 4-Hour Mapping Session
Mapped Process	High, Process Assumed Intricate, Only Partially Appreciated, High-Effort Mapping Required
Critical Process Identification	Extreme, Entire Processes Eliminated, New Processes Developed

Figure 4.1
Focal Process Model

Type

Action-Based
Workshop

Model

Focal Process   Issues   Actions   Presentation   Response

Process

Focal Process Well
Known in Advance
(begin where we are)

Process Cues Issue
Identification

Normal Action-Based
Workshop Model
Format

Figure 4.2
Process-Mapping Model

Type

Process
Mapping

Model

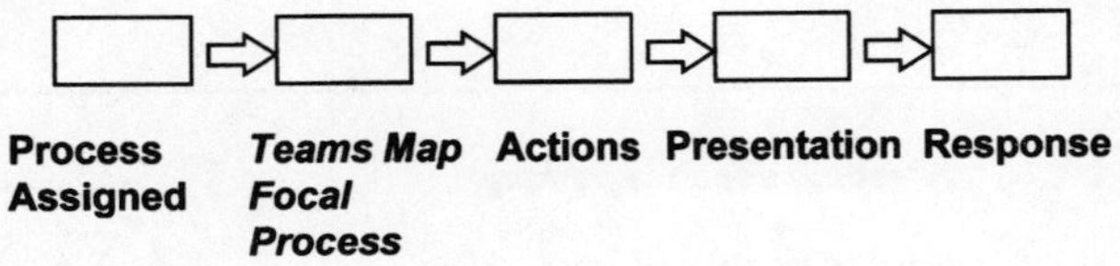

Process   Teams Map   Actions   Presentation   Response
Assigned   Focal
            Process

Process Comments

"Only the Analyzed
Can Analyze"

Accommodates General
Issues

Starts from Current
Situation

Labor Intensive

Figure 4.3
Mapped-Process Model

Mapped Process Model

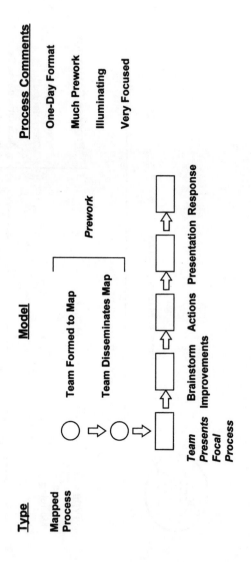

Type

Mapped
Process

Model

Team Formed to Map

Team Disseminates Map

Prework

Team Presents Focal Process

Brainstorm Improvements

Actions

Presentation

Response

Process Comments

One-Day Format

Much Prework

Illuminating

Very Focused

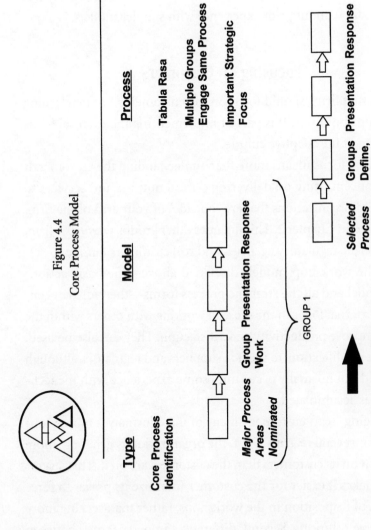

Figure 4.4
Core Process Model

Type

Core Process
Identification

Model

Major Process Group Presentation Response
Areas Work
Nominated

GROUP 1

Elaborating Process

Process

Tabula Rasa

Multiple Groups
Engage Same Process

Important Strategic
Focus

Selected Groups Presentation Response
Process Define,
Areas Refine,
Presented and Map

GROUP 2

ciple that I advocated in my book with Lawrence Hrebiniak; that is, select the strategy that accomplishes your objective with the least level of intervention. There are costs of over-intervening as well as of doing too little in change. This point should be kept in mind especially with the Core Process workshop model. This method will generally not be successful without prior experience with simpler models.

Focusing on Customers

The idea that firms should focus on the customer is not new. Doing something about it is. It is part of implementing the external focus dimension of the adaptive culture.

External focus means more than understanding the customer. It means concentrating on delivering critical outputs and services to groups and organizations that are "outside" of your area of the firm, as discussed in Chapter 2. This includes other groups *within* the firm, and suppliers, regulatory agencies, and real customers *outside* it.

All the workshop models discussed above—the basic action-based model and all the strategic process forms—therefore concentrate on external focus in the sense of working with others within the firm to improve productivity and satisfaction. They can also be used, with little modification, to include suppliers and regulators, although this would not normally occur until some experience with the techniques was accumulated.

Engaging "real" customers in any of these formats is more problematic for several reasons. First, the organization is generally more dependent on its customers than the customers are on it. This "asymmetry" makes it easier for the customer to utilize its power to force adoption of its position in the workshops, rather than seeking more cooperative solutions. Second, differences in perspectives between your organization and your customer's may not only be due to misunderstanding and a lack of a shared perspective. *There are likely to be situations in which there are genuine and significant conflicts*

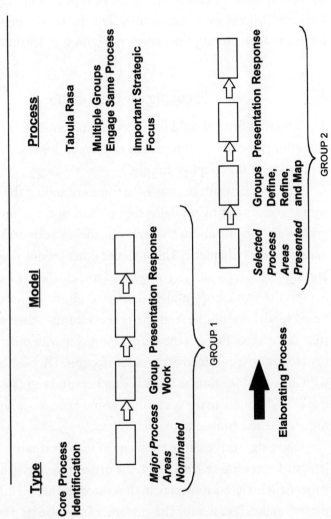

Figure 4.4
Core Process Model

ciple that I advocated in my book with Lawrence Hrebiniak; that is, select the strategy that accomplishes your objective with the least level of intervention. There are costs of over-intervening as well as of doing too little in change. This point should be kept in mind especially with the Core Process workshop model. This method will generally not be successful without prior experience with simpler models.

Focusing on Customers

The idea that firms should focus on the customer is not new. Doing something about it is. It is part of implementing the external focus dimension of the adaptive culture.

External focus means more than understanding the customer. It means concentrating on delivering critical outputs and services to groups and organizations that are "outside" of your area of the firm, as discussed in Chapter 2. This includes other groups *within* the firm, and suppliers, regulatory agencies, and real customers *outside* it.

All the workshop models discussed above—the basic action-based model and all the strategic process forms—therefore concentrate on external focus in the sense of working with others within the firm to improve productivity and satisfaction. They can also be used, with little modification, to include suppliers and regulators, although this would not normally occur until some experience with the techniques was accumulated.

Engaging "real" customers in any of these formats is more problematic for several reasons. First, the organization is generally more dependent on its customers than the customers are on it. This "asymmetry" makes it easier for the customer to utilize its power to force adoption of its position in the workshops, rather than seeking more cooperative solutions. Second, differences in perspectives between your organization and your customer's may not only be due to misunderstanding and a lack of a shared perspective. *There are likely to be situations in which there are genuine and significant conflicts between your interests and those of the customer.* Cooperation and clearing up misconceptions may make many of these disappear, but it may also be the case that you encounter genuine cases of disagreement at a more fundamental level.

Resolving these issues requires conflict management and negotiation at a higher level than in prior workshops. As a consequence, considerable prework is necessary before instituting a customer-focused workshop. An additional step needs to be added to establish a common ground for approaching these difficult issues and for clarifying what they are. Many concerns will evaporate in the face of information, and many problems will turn out not to be problems at all. However, some will remain and these issues will require the most energy for their solution.

Customer-focused workshops are generally facilitated by outside consultants. This is so for a number of reasons. Considerable skill is needed when conflicts occur. More important, the facilitator needs to be seen as an independent agent, capable of fairly responding to both sides of an issue. This type of workshop assumes a substantial amount of maturity in the use of the general action-based workshop concept, and should never be undertaken without substantial experience with simpler forms.

Workshop Models and the Adaptive Culture

Table 4.3 summarizes the impact of the action-based, strategic process, and customer-focused workshops on the dimensions of the adaptive culture. Simpler action-based workshops primarily addressed the *acting* and *cooperating* dimensions of the adaptive culture, and not the *thinking* dimensions.

It was necessary to walk before we could run. The basic concept behind all the workshop models is that "attitudes follow actions." This same principle applies to the overall sequence of cultural change activities. The workshops initially modeled the acting and cooper-

Table 4.3

Cultural Dimensions Addressed by Three Action-Based Workshop Models

Workshop Type	Adaptive Culture Dimensions							
	Thinking			Acting		Cooperating		
	External Focus	Process Focus	Ownership	Speed	Initiative	Collaboration	Non-political	Boundaryless
Action-based workshop			√	√	√	√	√	√
Strategic process workshop		√	√	√	√	√	√	√
Customer-focused workshop	√		√	√	√	√	√	√

ating dimensions. The change in organizational culture that resulted allowed the focus to shift to the thinking dimensions. This could not have occurred without new cultural expectations emphasizing fewer boundaries, initiative, and collaboration. Focusing on processes and customers crosses boundaries, requires collaboration, and involves taking initiative beyond immediate job responsibilities. Cultural change initially spreads from early action-based workshops to the broader organization (for the acting and cooperating dimensions), and then from strategic process and customer-focused workshops to the organization again (for the thinking dimensions). The new ways of thinking, acting, and cooperating—the norms, values, and beliefs of the adaptive culture—are established in this sequence of activities.

Hitting the Wall: Transitioning to Management-Driven Systems Change

Getting this far in *MegaChange* is an accomplishment. The culture is changing in very positive ways, and the organization is more productive than ever before. People are experiencing a new quality of work life—one based on their capabilities rather than on their presumed limitations—and are enjoying it.

Getting here has taken a substantial amount of work and commitment. Nothing that has been described above is "free." Managing in the new way has required more of everyone, but the gains have been worth it. It has taken from one to two years to get this far.

When Excitement Wanes

Unfortunately, many organizations encounter problems at this point. Just when real gains are being made, it seems as if many people have lost their steam. Excitement wanes, and workforce interest in empowerment seems endangered. The overall intervention seems to be "hitting the wall."

This does not signal any failure in the work done so far. It signals a need to proceed to the next, management-driven stages of large-scale changes in systems and structures. I will discuss structural change in the next chapter. The need for management-driven systems change and the typical forms that this takes are discussed below. It is important to remember that structural and systems change go hand in hand at this stage. Some of the systems issues discussed below are necessary to make the debureaucratized and process-centered structures presented in the next chapter operational.

What Causes Loss of Excitement?

Why do large-scale cultural change efforts often encounter problems at this point? After so much has been gained, shouldn't energy be at an all-time peak? Five factors combine to produce this counterintuitive result. It is important to understand these factors because they signal a need to go forward, rather than to rethink and repeat previous steps. They are critical to the *MegaChange* process because they are the indicators that the next major change sequence—management-driven systems and structural change—must begin immediately.

Novelty Wears Off

Large-scale change is challenging, and even frightening at times. Building organizations based on capabilities rather than limitations is appealing and novel. Each step forward in the process brings more efficacy, more self-control, and more involvement. This is, indeed, something new.

As experience with the new work methods and change process grows, what was once novel becomes more routine. The "meeting of a lifetime" becomes a part of the daily work culture. Change is exciting, and a perceived lack of novelty signals that it is time to move to the next stages of change.

People Get Tired

Although change is exciting, it is also a lot of work. Everyone has been asked to do more in the process. Existing objectives and responsibilities could not be neglected as new ones were invented and implemented. Although process simplification and the elimination of rules and bad procedures ultimately free people up, in the short run taking them out means more, rather than less, work.

At this point people have not yet experienced the full benefit of their accomplishments. Some changes are just coming on line, yet a great deal of effort has been expended. People are beginning to wonder when the change will be complete, just when the next major change sequence needs to begin.

A Process, Not a Program

The old top-down logic of change that characterized Stage I and II organizations was "programmatic" in nature. Change management was organized and run just like any other program to introduce a new product or to execute a project. Project management has an identifiable beginning and end. When the project is completed, the program is over, and people go back to their routine activities or begin another project.

Programmatic change efforts were appropriate in simpler times. Change activities could be concentrated in a project and executed, and the organization would then remain relatively stable for a long period of time. Stage I and II organizational forms utilized this programmatic logic of change. Hypercompetition, technological change, and the values imperative have rendered this logic obsolete, necessitating a process as opposed to programmatic orientation.

A process orientation emphasizes the ongoing and continuing nature of change. A change process may have a clear beginning, but it does not have a clearly defined ending point. It emphasizes broad directional goals as opposed to short-term specifics. It is more oriented toward developing an organization's ongoing capacity to change itself than in accomplishing a specific short-term change.

MegaChange emphasizes this process focus. It is aimed at creating an organization's ability to constantly renew and improve itself and to empower its members, based upon human capabilities rather than limitations. This is new to many people, because their past exposures in large-scale transitions have been driven by programmatic change logics based in Stage I and II organization types. As a consequence, they are expecting a short-term change effort that will be over in one or at most two years.

At this point, management must emphasize that change is a way of life, not an isolated event. Everyone is part of this change process. It will continue with all the challenge, effort, and excitement that has been experienced so far.

Inventing the Future

People also seem to lose motivation at this stage due to ambiguity about how to proceed to the next level. Although the approach advocated in this book is new, we *have* had the experience of the Human Relations, Participative Management, Quality of Work Life, Employee Involvement, and Total Quality movements as guides for our process thus far. Now, we are going far beyond their prescriptions, we are alone, and we don't know what to do.

The performance model concept from Chapter 3 predicts that without adequate understanding of our tasks we will falter. The principles outlined in this book provide this guidance, based on a large, rigorous, and relevant body of management research. Up until this point organizations have chosen to "go it alone" with respect to much of management theory. They will not get much further without it. Theory and practice work together in *MegaChange*.

Strategies, Structures, and Systems "Trip the Players"

"Sparky" Anderson, the famous major league baseball coach, was once asked, "Sparky, what makes you such a great coach?" He replied, "I don't trip the players when they run out onto the field." The workforce is empowered at this stage, but it continues to be "tripped up" by old structures and systems that get in the way of the new culture. Some of these can and have been changed on the basis of workforce-driven change initiatives, as described above. Others require management-driven change (on the basis of the knowledge-based empowerment principle) and *have not been addressed yet*. These structures and systems are now impediments to change, and the workforce is expecting management to change, just as they have. Expectations are high, and when they are not met, frustration results.

Critical Actions at the "Hitting the Wall" Stage

Management must do five things at this stage, as shown in Table 4.4. First, it must communicate that the loss of novelty is a sign of accomplishment and not failure. It is a sign that we have mastered the first major steps in change and now must go on to the next stages. This is a new and exciting challenge.

Second, it is important that management recognize that people are tired and emphasize the gains that have been made and that are just beginning to come on line. The workforce is probably just beginning to experience some of the benefits from actions taken in the past. This lagging nature of the effects of change—work now, payoff later—has to be highlighted. It also has to be the case that people receive the payoff!

The Human Relations efforts failed when the workforce realized that despite all the rhetoric, the entire process was largely a tool for productivity enhancement. It was not aimed at the higher standard—productivity through meaningful work—described in Chapter 1.

Table 4.4

"Hitting the Wall"

Critical Change Factors for Advancing to the Next Stages of *MegaChange*

Problem	Critical Change Factor
Novelty wears off	Loss of novelty indicates mastery of first steps, now signals move to next major Stage of *MegaChange*
People get tired	Quality of work life must improve, emphasize efforts, lead payoffs in intervention
Process, not a program	Change as a way of life, management models, commitment
Inventing the future	Outline *MegaChange* philosophy, process for future steps
Systems and structures "trip the players"	Management changes itself, initiates enabling systems

More and more work to achieve someone else's goals is not palatable. Continued, sustained effort requires more.

At this point gains must be seen in the quality of work life. The effects of change lag behind the actions undertaken to produce them. To the workforce this means that the work has been done, but they have not yet received the payoff. The positive effects of change, ones that will be emotionally important to the workforce, must be highlighted and embraced by management as the changes begin to come on line. The workforce must experience what is has worked for.

Third, management must communicate the importance of change as a way of life. The management actions advocated at the beginning of Chapter 3 can serve as a model here. Management must continue to display emotion for change, embrace it in the strategy and mission, provide resources to support it, and constantly provide the rationale for continued change. The method-as-model principle is strictly relevant: management must model the behaviors and culture that everyone is striving for.

Fourth, the process of *MegaChange* must be understood by everyone. Managing large-scale cultural change is very complex. It is important that the major steps in change be appreciated by everyone. When this happens, people understand *where* they stand in the process. We must make it clear that no one has all of the answers, but that everyone is engaged in finding the solutions. You are not alone. We will continue to make progress.

Finally, management-driven change of systems and structures must begin now. The workforce is increasingly handicapped by existing practices. They have changed, but management has not really begun to change itself. Many transitions fail at this point. Being "boundaryless" means sharing in the change process. It is not something management does to the workforce, it is something that they do with the workforce. Each has a role to play based upon the knowledge-based empowerment principle.

Managing Large Systems Changes in the Latter Stages of *MegaChange*

Three factors require management-driven change in systems (and in structures, to be discussed in the next chapter). These are problems of *consistency, resources,* and *expertise.* The first two, consistency and resources, are the same problems encountered in what I called the "discretion problems" above. Many human resource and information systems require consistency in application, and may be quite costly as well. Someone has to implement this consistency and legitimate the expenditure of resources. Both of these problems can be handled using the procedures described in the sections dealing with workforce-driven large systems change. The problem of expertise cannot.

The workforce has the most knowledge of local rules, processes, and systems implementation issues. Management, in contrast, has the most knowledge of the design of overall structures and systems. Obviously these roles are complementary. However, it is management who has the most training, experience, and knowledge of the *overall* architecture of structures and systems. This is, after all, what they get paid to do. They will be the key drivers of change in this instance, in accordance with the knowledge-based empowerment principle.

Two "Dilemmas" of *MegaChange*

There are two dilemmas of change that require management-driven large systems change. Both of these require reinventing human resource systems.

The Dilemma of Contingency without Control

This is a very interesting problem that arises in organizations that have de-layered and widened management spans of control. In Stage I and II organizations, the "optimal" span of control was believed to be between five and seven workers per manager. When layers of management are reduced, this span usually increases, even with downsizing. Reforming and debureaucratizing structures involves intelligently de-layering organizations, resulting in wider spans of control. This allows the workforce appropriate freedom to exercise their new empowerment, but it poses a new problem.

The dilemma is this. With wider spans, management has less oversight of each individual worker. Spans of control of 50 or more are not uncommon today. This is consistent with more workforce autonomy, but poses a new problem. Research is very clear that a contingency between performance and rewards is necessary for the rewards to have a motivational impact.[3] How can this contingency be established when the manager does not have complete knowledge of each worker's contributions? This is the essence of the "contingency without control" dilemma.

360° Performance Appraisals: Resolving "Contingency without Control"

Resolving the dilemma requires a large-scale management-driven change in the performance appraisal system. The solution is "360° performance appraisals."[4] If management cannot reliably assure contingency, and if this contingency is important, then someone else must do it. The solution is to use additional raters for this purpose.

The 360° metaphor means using a set of raters that "surrounds" the person whose performance is being appraised. Their performance would be rated by their supervisors, by their peers, by their subordinates (if they exist), and by themselves. There is a substantial literature in industrial psychology detailing how this process should be conducted.[5] This work is almost never utilized in practice, however, due to ignorance. Many problems can be avoided through understanding of the subtle points that are important in this process. In general, 360° performance appraisals are superior to normal ratings in terms of their reliability, validity, and ability to predict future performance, and they are entirely consistent with debureaucratized structures. A significant proportion of compensation—performance-contingent pay—should be based upon 360° performance appraisals.[6]

The Dilemma of Careers without Hierarchy

Debureaucratized and de-layered structures also pose another dilemma. With fewer levels of hierarchy, there are fewer management jobs. Yet most of us define success in our careers as progress upward in the organization. Careers are vitally important to us. How can we have a career with very limited opportunities to move up in the organization? This is the "careers without hierarchy" dilemma.

A career is a meaningful sequence of job experiences.[7] Making work more meaningful produces radical gains in productivity and satisfaction. In adaptive organizations there are more opportunities for meaningful work, and therefore real careers, than in other organization forms. However, without extensive hierarchy, people must understand a career in the important sense above, rather than only as a series of promotions.

Lateral Careers and Skill-Based Pay: Resolving "Progression without Promotion"

Careers become more lateral in *MegaChange*. People may move through positions horizontally, learning new skills, facing new challenges, and gaining more expertise. In Stage III organizations, influence and status are accorded to those who are most knowledgeable and skilled. Progressing in a career means receiving more influence due to expertise rather than hierarchical rank. This is very desirable because of the knowledge-based empowerment principle. As people become more expert we want them to have more influence in organizational decision making and action. Power should drive knowledge. This is not always the case with hierarchical power. Often those with the most influence are those with the least knowledge of the problems at hand. Lateral careers are consistent with empowering the workforce through knowledge.

De-layering often takes place as a way to cut costs, lowering the denominator in the productivity equation (I will discuss this in greater detail in Chapter 5). With de-layering people still want careers, but must find them laterally. When people develop skills in multiple areas, they expect to be compensated for their greater value to the organization. But the same cost-cutting mentality that led to the de-layering in the first place says that their pay cannot be increased. After all, it would raise costs! This is an excellent illustration of how undertaking change efforts for the wrong reasons leads to fundamental problems with implementation. Productivity is not just about costs. It is also about revenues—revenues that are generated by a motivated and engaged workforce. We cannot reach the higher standard discussed in Chapter 1 by focusing on costs alone.

MegaChange produces higher levels of productivity and satisfaction through meaningful work for everyone. Cost cutting is not the goal of *MegaChange.* Hence, as the workforce learns to have alternative careers in the new Stage III de-layered structures, there is no fundamental inconsistency between rewarding people for skill and expertise gains and the overall goals of transformation. Equity theory[8] demands that people who are more highly skilled are also compensated more highly. This means that pay systems should include a component of compensation based upon expertise—skill-based pay.[9] Overall pay would be the sum of *skill-based* pay and *performance-contingent* pay determined using the 360° performance appraisal process.

Summary

This chapter has presented a set of concepts, actions, and tools for engaging systems. The focus for engaging systems is on the thinking dimensions of the adaptive culture. The actions taken at this stage must support strategic goals, enable earlier steps, and model the new culture. Modeling the ownership dimension of the desired culture also means that outside consultants play a very diminished role in engaging systems, as they did in earlier steps.

The knowledge-based empowerment concept is the key concept of this chapter. It tells us what the roles of management and the workforce are in the early, middle, and latter stages of engaging systems. In general, the early and middle stages are workforce-driven and the latter stages are management-driven. It also clarifies the very important differences between empowerment and delegation, and emphasizes ownership instead of assigned responsibility.

Actions addressing critical change factors in the early stages of engaging systems addressed four types of problems. These were termed "bad," "historical," "maligned," and "discretion problem" issues. In the middle stages, actions focus on processes and customers.

Four modifications of the action-based workshop were developed for improving processes. These were the Focal Process, Process Mapping, Mapped Process, and Core Process workshops. The customer-focused workshop involved customers in problem solving and negotiation around key issues of joint concern.

A problem that occurs in the middle stages of change was identified as "hitting the wall." It describes the condition in which change activities seem to be running down. The causes of this condition were identified. Overcoming them requires management to signal the move to the next stage of *MegaChange,* to allow people to benefit from the change, to emphasize the process as opposed to the program nature of the effort, to outline future steps, and to begin changing itself and not only the workforce.

When these steps are accomplished, the organization enters the latter stages of *MegaChange.* These are concerned with large-scale changes in structures and strategies. Management-driven changes in structures (to be discussed in the next chapter) require supporting changes in systems. Two dilemmas—contingency without control and careers without promotions—are posed by de-layering and debureaucratizing structures. These necessitate 360° performance appraisals, lateral careers, and making compensation contingent on both job performance and skill.

This concludes our discussion of the concepts, actions, and tools for engaging systems. The next step focuses on the logic of debureaucratizing and reforming structures. Some of these ideas have already been alluded to. It is now time to discuss them systematically.

Reforming Structures

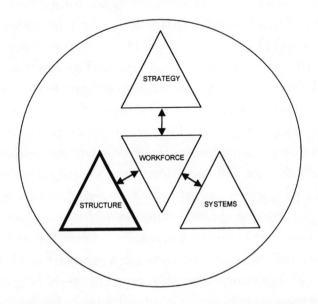

The previous chapter discussed the concepts, actions, and tools for implementing radical changes in organizational systems. The next stage in *MegaChange* is reforming structures. Policies, processes, and systems all exist in the context of the organization's structure. Changes in systems require enabling changes in structures to remove barriers that hinder performance in the new workplace. Changes in structure are also necessary to directly support the goals of the change effort. This chapter introduces the ideas that are necessary to accomplish these purposes. It concludes with an extended analysis of the Price Waterhouse structural transformation project.

Restructuring, Reengineering, and Reforming Structures

Many organizations have attempted some variety of transformation in the past decade, often with very poor results. Most of these efforts have had a strong structural content. "Restructuring" has been the dominant form of change. In restructuring, firms have been downsized, de-layered, and "right"-sized. These efforts have been direct manipulations of the fundamental structural configuration of the firm. The logics of change, content, and configuration employed in restructuring violate almost every principle advanced in this book. Change was top down with little or no workforce participation. There were few if any adjustments in other systems to support the structural changes, and no recognition of the critical interdependencies among strategy, structure, systems, and the workforce. The content was narrow, focusing almost exclusively on size, levels of hierarchy, and, as a consequence, spans of control. Having failed at implementing Stage II organizations, management retreated to Stage I thinking—regressing rather than progressing—hoping that the solution to their problems lay in returning to the familiar bureaucratic model. It is no surprise that this approach, monumentally at odds with changes in values, technology, competitive realities, and theory, has failed.

Reengineering, like restructuring, was also bred in desperation. Organizations were failing. The first attempt to cope—restructuring—did not work. The second attempt was reengineering—to rethink every system, structure, and process from the ground up. The goal was radical gains in productivity.

Statistics indicate that approximately 65 percent of reengineering efforts fail.[1] It is instructive and worthwhile to consider why reengineering attempts experience such high failure rates. Reengineering does recognize the important interdependencies between strategy, structure, and systems. It is much more powerful than restructuring

in this regard. In terms of content, reengineering incorporates many Stage II ideas such as a focus on lateral coordination and teamwork, which can be powerful when implemented correctly.[2]

Reengineering, however, is subverted by the hidden assumptions that it is based upon. The goal is productivity, and not the higher standard of performance (productivity through meaningful work) advanced in Chapter 1. It sets its sights too low, and delivers on them, sometimes. Despite using the word "empowerment" frequently, reengineering adopts a fundamental machine logic of organization that is inconsistent with participation. When people obstruct change, it is not seen as a failure of the process. Instead, it signals their need to be "warehoused" or "bought off" to remove their objections. This hardly models empowerment. Finally, the process is consultant-driven, and not management- and workforce-driven. It is something that is done to people and not with them. It is implemented in a top-down manner by consultants whose methodologies make it clear that empowerment means going along "or else."

Restructuring and reengineering are very much at odds with the ideas presented in this book. They promise overnight success and radical improvements in performance, build upon skills that are familiar to every manager, and require very little change in management behavior. It is no wonder they have been so popular. It is no wonder they have such a high failure rate.

I have chosen the word "reforming" to signal a break with this type of thinking. We cannot get to the future by acting in the old way and covering up our hesitancy with new language. Restructuring and reengineering are just the old logic in new clothes. Reforming the corporation means getting on with the business of change and embracing new ways of thinking, acting, and cooperating—the *adaptive culture.*

Reforming structures alters structures in a manner consistent with the *new logic of change* as developed in Chapter 2. This means building structures based upon capabilities rather than limitations (the capability assumption), obtaining performance by creating meaningful work (aspiring to a higher standard), engaging everyone in the transformation (utilizing the top-down–bottom-up change logic), modeling the culture we are striving for (the method-as-model concept), and assigning key roles in the process based upon knowledge, ability, and motivation (knowledge-based empowerment). The solution and results obtained will be unlike anything produced by restructuring and reengineering.

The following sections develop the concepts, actions, and tools for reforming structures in detail. Following a brief discussion of workforce-driven structural change, I discuss the *debureaucratization model*. This is the major concept introduced in this chapter. The model is then applied to indicate the critical change factors at the middle and later stages of reforming structures, along with tools for implementing these actions. As in earlier steps, structural change must *support* the firm's strategy, *enable* its systems to function appropriately, and *model* the desired culture of the firm.

Reforming Structure in the Early Stages of Change

Reforming structure is predominantly an activity at the middle and later stages of the *MegaChange* process. However, some structural change does take place in earlier stages. Action-based workshops cover many topics as part of the empowerment process. Most of these issues are concerned with local rules and human resources concerns, but some structural topics arise. Many of these structural concerns are "discretion problem" types of issues, and they should be handled in the same way that they were for systems changes (see Chapter 3 and the discussion of work/family concerns). However, some structural problems can be addressed within the framework of the action-based workshop.

The issues that can be handled within a workshop are generally of three types. First, there are "workgroup composition" issues. These arise in a workshop when it becomes obvious that for a group to execute its responsibilities it requires skills that are not represented in the group. They may exist elsewhere and need to be relocated to this group.

There may also be "group responsibilities" problems. In this case, it is not clear which group is responsible for what. Deciding who should take the lead in particular stages of the process being discussed will resolve this problem.

Finally, there are "capabilities" problems. Often, people will point to particular capabilities that they believe the organization must have to better execute its mission. Many times when this happens, the capabilities exist in the organization but are unknown to the group. In other cases they have to be developed.

All of these issues concern structure, and share the common property of being able to be fit into the context of a workshop format. The majority of structural decisions are so broad, however, that they do not lend themselves easily to resolution using this tool. Some can be handled using the procedures for discretion problem issues, discussed earlier. However, the concerns of workforce-driven change activities are ordinarily local. What is on your mind is usually what you have most direct experience with. The broader issues of overall organization structure are distant and unfamiliar in many cases, except to management, suggesting that the next stages of reforming structure should be management-driven. Understanding the critical actions at this stage requires understanding of the core concept of this chapter, the debureaucratization model.

The Debureaucratization Model

In order to understand *de*bureaucratization it is necessary to first understand bureaucratization. Bureaucratization was a Stage I organizing activity. Debureaucratizing is a Stage III organizing activity.

The basic structure of virtually every organization is bureaucratic.[3] Sometimes we fool ourselves with cleverly drawn organization charts that avoid the familiar boxes and lines, but the elements of basic structure still remain. The objective of debureaucratization is not the elimination of all structure. This would create anarchy. The objective is the right amount of structure. Debureaucratization doesn't mean disorganization.

The Logic of Basic Structure

A basic structure has five key elements and a foundation objective, as shown in Figure 5.1. The foundation objective is the task that has to be performed. In order to accomplish this task, a basic structure is required. The five elements of this basic structure are: departmentation, rules, delegation, hierarchy, and span of control.

These elements are not new. They were a key part of Stage I thinking. However, it was not until recently that management appreciated the important relationships among them.[4,5,6] The logic of basic structure specifies the content and sequence of debureaucratization actions and derives from these relationships. It may be stated in the following important way:

> Logically, each element of basic structure solves an organizing problem posed by the one coming before it. In so doing, it creates a new problem of its own. This "new" problem must then be addressed by the next step in organizing, and so on until the basic organizing process is complete.

Designing Basic Structures: Applying the Logic

Applying this logic to the elements of basic organization described above results in the following process for designing basic structure. The first step is forming *departments* based upon the *tasks* to be

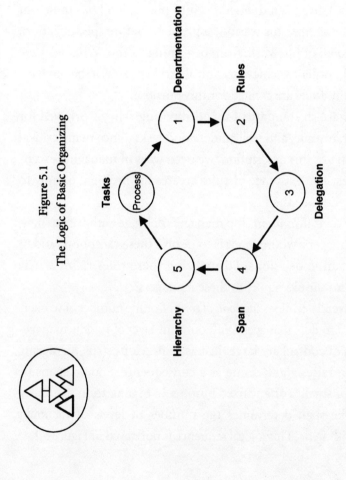

Figure 5.1
The Logic of Basic Organizing

Departmentation

Rules

Delegation

Span

Hierarchy

Tasks

Process

1

2

3

4

5

Self-Contained

Deviation
Amplifying

Task Driven

performed. The organizing problem at this step is "Who should do what?" Generally, the answer to this question is to specialize the labor so that people can become expert at parts of the overall task, improving technical competence. Structurally, departments are formed on the basis of expertise by grouping people with similar expertise together.

Solving this first problem, however, actually creates the next. Once the work has been divided up into pieces, it all has to be put back together again. This was not a problem before specialization. Everyone did all of the work, from beginning to end. What we have taken apart in order to achieve technical excellence has to be put back together again. *Rules* are created for this purpose.

Rules establish standards for coordinating. They work well for simple, clear, routine, and well-understood tasks. Since many critical activities don't fit this description, we need ways of managing exceptions to rules. The existence of rules creates the problem of how to resolve exceptions to them.

The answer is *delegation.* Top managers delegate authority to new, "middle" managers, whose job it is to resolve these exceptions and to make nonroutine decisions. Formalizing these roles raises a new question. Who should report to these managers?

The answer determines the *span of control,* or the number of workers reporting to a middle manager. With only one layer of middle management, spans of control are large. Just as in previous steps, answering one question raises another one as a consequence. Should spans be made large or small? For any fixed number of organization members, specifying the span determines the number of levels of *hierarchy* by simple arithmetic. This logical sequence is portrayed in Figure 5.1.

Basic Structure and the Growth of Bureaucracy

This logic has some very interesting properties. First, it shows that all of the steps for creating basic structures are highly interdependent.

Since each step builds upon the one preceding it, and that one on the step before, *the process is deviation-amplifying*. A mistake at the beginning of the process builds throughout the entire sequence. If we do not specify the tasks correctly, we form bad departments, coordinate them with excess rules, and so on. By the time we reach the end of the basic organizing process, small errors have become large ones. Getting the early steps right is therefore essential.

Second, once the basic tasks are determined, *the process is relatively self-contained*. Choices at each step depend upon decisions made at the preceding one. They are not directly influenced by outside variables. The correct choice of rules for coordinating your departments depends upon what these departments are, not on what the competition is doing. Imitation may be the sincerest form of flattery, but it is bad organization design. You organize to execute *your* mission, not someone else's.

Finally, and perhaps as a consequence of the previous two properties, *the process is heavily task-driven*. If the process is self-contained and deviation-amplifying, having an effective structure requires starting with a clear task and systematically building a basic structure to implement it. Adjusting elements of basic structure on a piecemeal basis without recognizing the logic of bureaucratization invites disaster. That is precisely what has happened in many organizations: restructuring de-layered and expanded spans of control without paying attention to any of the steps in basic organizing that should have preceded these actions.

These properties explain the unnecessary growth of bureaucracy and its unfortunate consequences. The scenario goes like this. We specify our tasks poorly and create departments to do the wrong things. Poor rules are created to coordinate unnecessary activities. These errors are amplified and it becomes apparent that the basic structure is too bureaucratized. When this happens we try to fix it by directly adjusting one element in the process, such as layers or spans of control. These do not fit the basic tasks we are trying to accomplish.

A lot of people lose their jobs inappropriately. Things only get worse. Costs go up instead of down. We look for a new job.

Debureaucratization is required in situations like the one described in the preceding paragraph. Excessive bureaucracy may also result from more "evolutionary" processes. Structures are created to accomplish the core tasks of the organization, as described above. As these tasks shift, structures that were once very appropriate no longer serve the firm. Small adjustments are made to correct deficiencies. Parts of the structure that were needed to execute the old mission still exist despite their irrelevance to the new tasks. We are running two organizations: one to do what is necessary and an older one that is no longer needed. Coordinating the unnecessary units generates unnecessary rules and hierarchy. More hierarchy means more managers and levels. The problem is exacerbated by the deviation-amplifying properties of the basic organizing process, resulting in more and more unnecessary bureaucracy.

Debureaucratization and Cultural Change

The logic and examples in the preceding discussion make it clear that ongoing structural change will be a permanent part of managing in the future. Tasks will be constantly changing in response to competitive and technological shifts. Organizations must be quick to remove unneeded old structures and to develop new ones that respond to the tasks at hand without creating excessive bureaucracy. Doing this means constantly *reforming* basic structures from the beginning of the sequence described above.

This is a rather frightening thought for those of us who were once accustomed to thinking of structure as something permanent. Reforming structures will occur with greater and greater frequency. Reforming structures is radical. It does not allow for patching up the old structure.

It should be apparent why reforming structures occupies this place in the sequence of change activities. How can structural change at this rate ever be possible in Stage I or II cultures that emphasize control and oversight, complexity and conformance, and rigidity and routinization? The obvious answer is that it cannot be. Reforming structures needs *process* knowledge and fewer *boundaries* to reform departments, *collaboration* to reduce rules, *ownership* to minimize unneeded management, and *initiative* to replace direction and widen spans. These are the dimensions of the adaptive culture. Minimizing bureaucracy means first building a culture that allows debureaucratization. Changes in competition and technology require radical changes in structure. The values imperative discussed in Chapter 1 requires that these "reformations" respect individuals' desires for meaningful work and efficacy. Reforming structures is impossible without having first established the adaptive culture and having completed the steps in the preceding two chapters.

Debureaucratization:
Building Process-Driven Structures

The actions for debureaucratizing structures correspond exactly to each of the steps in basic organizing. The first three critical change factors are reducing departmentation, eliminating rules, and expanding roles, and they occur at the middle stages of change. Together, they create process-driven structures.

These decisions are interdependent as described above, and begin with departmentation based upon the task. For debureaucratization to occur we have to broaden the idea of task to include processes as well as goals. Bureaucratic structures focus on goals to the exclusion of the processes used to obtain them. Debureaucratization requires building a process orientation into the basic structure of the firm. Reducing departmentation, eliminating rules, and expanding roles are the actions for accomplishing this. Each of these is discussed separately below.

Reducing Departmentation through Process Focus

Departments are formed by placing the people who are the most interdependent with one another in a common group. This allows direct face-to-face communication among them and facilitates coordination. In Stage I and II organizations, specialization meant that these interdependencies were usually functional. That is, a whole piece of work was broken down into a number of smaller, more specialized pieces. Each of these had a specific "function" in relation to the whole. Putting them back together again was the obvious first priority, or the point of greatest interdependence. Doing so created a functional structure.

Work was specialized on the basis of goals. Each piece had a function in relation to achieving the overall goal or objective, and these functions were hierarchically structured. Each specialized piece was further specialized. For example, building an airplane requires engineering. Engineering is specialized into aerodynamics, structures, and design. Aerodynamics is further specialized into stability and control and performance work, and each of these has smaller specialties such as flight test and wind tunnel investigations. Flight test and wind tunnel work are highly interdependent and must be coordinated to do performance work, so they are departmentalized in a group called Performance Assessment, or some similar name. This is a functional work group.

The specialization logic for the most part ignored the processes necessary to integrate what were becoming increasingly fragmented parts of the whole. The current interest in process-driven structures is a testimony to the fact that structure often split key processes at the wrong places. Specialization helped achieve technical excellence, but it made coordination and integration very difficult,[7] and produced excessive bureaucracy.

Building a process focus into structures can eliminate unnecessary bureaucracy. The foundation objective for a process-driven structure is a process rather than the overall goal. That is not to say that process-driven structures neglect goals. Obviously they cannot, or they would be useless. However, rather than basing structure directly on goals, process-driven organizations base structure on critical processes[8] derived from goals, as shown in Figure 5.2. This has the desirable characteristic of building a process orientation directly into the basic structure of the organizations, initially through the formation of departments. Stage II organizations do this after the fact, in a kind of patch-up mode. The basic structure is still largely functional, but a process perspective is added on top of this basic structure in the form of teams or task forces.

Goal specialization produced functional organizations that neglected processes. Processes and functions are both critical to achieving goals. Neglecting processes will result in structures in which the logic of specialization dominates without the countervailing logic

Figure 5.2
Debureaucratization: Reducing Departmentation

RATIONALE:
Group activities that are most interdependent to facilitate coordination around key processes

PROBLEM:
Lack of process knowledge leads to errors

A   B   C

unnecessary group

ACTION:
Reduce Departmentation
  Fewer depart = fewer boundaries
  Process understanding reduces need to coordinate departments
  Natural DOL reduces unnecessary jobs, checkers

TOOLS:
Process mapping

of process focus. Stage II organizations correct for this tendency, but building both process and functional orientations into the structure as early in the organizing process as possible is desirable. This means keeping processes in mind during the formation of basic structures. Keeping processes in mind will reduce departmentation because it means that the logic of specialization must be assessed in the context of the costs it generates. These costs are the costs of coordination generated by excessive fragmentation of critical work processes.

The *action* for reducing departmentation is forming departments based on good process understanding. Therefore, taking this step depends on having identified and improved the core processes during the engaging systems stage of change, as well as upon management's vision of how these processes must evolve in the future. The *tool* for accomplishing this is process mapping executed within the format of the strategic process workshop models. These have been discussed extensively in Chapter 4, along with the critical steps for implementing them. Without good process understanding, the logic of specialization will dominate, and we are very likely to create too many departments.

Reducing departmentation reduces complexity and bureaucracy. Fewer departments means fewer boundaries. Better process understanding also reduces the need for structural coordination and specialized coordinating "departments" like liaison groups. Keeping processes in mind facilitates job enlargement and keeps the logical forces for specialization in check. A more natural and holistic division of labor reduces unnecessary jobs, such as those created to check on the work of others and which have no other function.

Eliminating Rules

Rules proliferate when there is excessive departmentation. Excessive departmentation can result from the forces described above, or for the "historical" reasons discussed in the previous sections. Departments that once made sense may not make sense in light of new goals and processes for achieving them. When there are too many departments, there are too many rules. Correcting errors in departmentation will leave excess rules, and these must be eliminated, as shown in Figure 5.3.

Rules were addressed earlier in the engaging systems step of change. At that stage rules were eliminated to enable workforce empowerment to proceed. Rules must change here to support as well as enable new tasks and revitalized processes. Earlier changes in rules were workforce-driven. Changes at this stage are more management-driven, consistent with the knowledge-based empowerment principle.

The *action* for reducing rules is management-driven rules elimination. This would occur following changes in departmentation and would utilize an action-based workshop format. Management would focus the workshop using a *tool* called the RAMMP[9] matrix. This is a simple device that aids the brainstorming portion of the workshop by

Figure 5.3
Debureaucratization: Eliminating Rules

RATIONALE:
Rules used to coordinate routine activities between groups

PROBLEM:
Rules proliferate with too many groups; red tape results when rules developed for non-necessary coordination

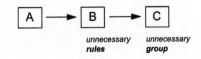

unnecessary rules   unnecessary group

ACTION:
Rule Elimination

    Eliminate "historical" rules
    Eliminate conflicting rules
    Revalidate suspect rules
    Eliminate unnecessary rules

TOOLS:
RAMMP Matrix

asking participants to identify non-value-added Reports, Approvals, Meetings, Measures, and Policies in the context of the new departmentation scheme.

Role Expansion

Too many departments led to too many rules. Exceptions to these rules had to be managed. The way that was accomplished was to assign these responsibilities to middle managers. Too many rules generated too many exceptions, and as a consequence too many managers, as shown in Figure 5.4.

When this happens some of the work that should be done by workers is done by managers, simply because there are too many of them and they need something to do. "Micro"-management results. Managers have too much time on their hands and spend it doing the wrong things. The solution is to eliminate excessive management positions and expand the responsibilities of both management and the workforce. Role expansion will enrich the jobs of both as a consequence.

This may sound peculiar. It is clear that if the workforce has more influence over their work they will be more empowered. But how can this also be true for managers if some management jobs are eliminated in the process? The answer is simple: management will do fewer of the things that it should not be doing and that should be done by others. Fewer managers will mean more *real* managerial work to be done for those who remain. Some of the people that have been pretending to do managerial work can stop pretending and get on with having a more meaningful career. Since the change process is based upon capabilities and engages everyone, people will have a chance to shape how their work develops and to manage this difficult transition. Basing the changes on the debureaucratization model ensures that the changes are not arbitrary and capricious. They are

Figure 5.4
Debureaucratization: Role Expansion

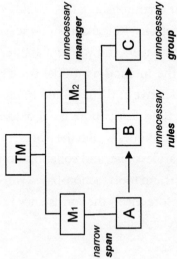

RATIONALE:

Middle management positions created to manage rules

PROBLEM:

Too many rules generate too many exceptions requiring too many managers for resolution

ACTION:

Role Expansion

Necessary coordination achieved
Doesn't presume omniscience
Total influence profile increased
Capabilities utilized
Power drives knowledge

TOOLS:

Role Negotiations

embedded in business purposes and a change process in which everyone has been heard. Meeting higher performance standards requires meaningful work for everyone, not only the workforce. No one likes to pretend, at least not for long.

The *action* for accomplishing this is role expansion. An effective *tool* is role negotiations. Role expansion means changing responsibilities for both managers and workers. Rather than assigning these responsibilities, the method-as-model principle requires that the process we use to arrive at them should model the end state we are trying to achieve. Role negotiations is a tool that meets this criterion. Negotiating responsibilities within the workgroup models ownership, initiative, boundarylessness, and collaboration. It is also consistent with earlier actions and tools (action-based workshops) in the change process, and therefore meets the consistency criteria advanced at the beginning of this chapter.

Role Negotiations

The concept of role negotiations was introduced into organizational design by Jay Galbraith.[10,11] There are three steps in the process. Participants first construct a matrix that summarizes the various actions and decisions for which responsibility will be negotiated. Following this, there is a discussion of what it means to be responsible. Several alternative varieties of responsibility are identified. Finally, the group actually negotiates who is going to be responsible for what. Each of these steps is discussed in greater detail below.

1. **Construction of the Responsibility Matrix:** In this step, participants define the rows and columns of the Responsibility Matrix. Each row is assigned one decision or action issue; the potential "responsibilities." The column headings are the positions or names of the participants in the process. Usually the matrix is formed on the basis of interviews conducted before

the actual meeting to negotiate responsibilities. Constructing the matrix is difficult, since often people are unaware of what the critical decisions are that must be made. Clarifying these can therefore be quite useful. The first step of the actual meeting is to review this chart and agree on exactly what is being negotiated.

2. **Discussion of what "responsibility" means:** After the group understands exactly what is meant by each of the decisions shown on the responsibility chart, there is a discussion of what it means to be "responsible." Responsibility means more here than in the traditional sense. Four types of responsibility are normally distinguished, though more may be desirable in particular situations. They are as follows:

Responsible: This person *initiates* the decision in the first place.

Approves: This person *approves* a decision made by another.

Consulted: This person must be *consulted before* the decision can be made.

Informed: This person must be *informed after* a decision has been made.

These four types of responsibility are signified on the matrix using the first letter of their names, **R, A, C,** or **I.**

3. **Responsibilities are negotiated:** In this step participants decide who is going to be responsible for what, and in what ways. There are a number of ways to approach this. One way is for each group member to complete the responsibility matrix and then aggregate the results. The group negotiates responsibilities for issues where there is not very much consensus. Another way is to analyze each issue one by one, without any overall balloting. At this stage of the change process, an open discussion like this should work well.

This is not the case when the technique is used in top-down change efforts.

Generally, each row of the matrix is filled out sequentially by the group. Undesirable patterns of responsibility are detected in this process. For example, a row in the matrix that contains no R's indicates a decision for which no one is responsible. Decisions like this will often not be made, or will be made so late that they become poor decisions. For role expansion, it should be the case that the group owns most of the decisions. The manager should have only a few R's and A's and even fewer C's. Figure 5.5 shows a bureaucratic responsibility matrix and contrasts that with one showing relative responsibilities after role expansion.

Following role expansion, managers should have fewer (but more appropriate) responsibilities within the group. They will be performing less micro-management as a consequence. They make fewer of the group's decisions for them, retain approval for only key items, and have fewer decisions for which they must be consulted. Surprisingly, research indicates that most managers prefer this situation. Although the *extent* of their roles within the group is diminished, the *content* of their work is enriched. They do fewer of the things that should be done by others and more of the things that they should do. Moreover, the group is now larger due to widened spans of control, the next step in the debureaucratization process.

Debureaucratization: Increasing Spans and De-layering

Restructuring attempts have often started with downsizing, or reducing the number of people in organizations in order to reduce

Figure 5.5
Responsibility Matrices Before and After Role Expansion

DEC \ MAKER	Manager	Worker 1	Worker 2	Worker 3
Decision 1	R	C	I	
Decision 2	R	I	C	I
Decision 3	A	I		
Decision 4	R	C		C
Decision 5	C		I	
Decision 6	A	I	C	

**Bureaucratic
Responsibility Matrix**

DEC \ MAKER	Manager	Worker 1	Worker 2	Worker 3
Decision 1	I	C	R	
Decision 2	C	R		I
Decision 3	A	I	R	
Decision 4	R	C		C
Decision 5	C		I	
Decision 6	I		C	R

**Responsibility Matrix with
Role Expansion**

costs. De-layering and widening spans is also part of reforming structures, but the purpose is not cost reduction. The purpose is to build organizational capability through the creation of meaningful work (the higher performance standard of Chapter 1). As I have already discussed, it is impossible to do this without simultaneously increasing productivity and satisfaction, far more important goals than cost reduction. Restructuring was aimed only at eliminating costs. Reforming structures increases revenues as well as reducing costs, and it does it in a way that builds and sustains workforce commitment and engagement. Achieving this requires us to use the logic of debureaucratization rather than the logic of cost reduction. This means that actions to widen spans and minimize levels should follow the earlier steps for building process-driven structures. Manipulating them outside of this context invites the kind of results experienced by "quick fix" restructuring efforts.

Increasing Spans

Increasing spans of control results naturally from role expansion, as shown in Figure 5.6. The workforce is doing more, freeing managers to really manage as opposed to supervising. Spans of control should be widened to ensure that everyone stays focused on this new and more appropriate division of labor. With wider spans of control managers do not have time to micro-manage, and the workforce cannot rely on them for things that they really should be doing themselves.

This method of widening spans of control should be contrasted with the methods used in Stage I and II organizations. Wider spans have always been desirable because they result in flatter organizations, and flatter organizations shorten critical communication paths between layers of the firm. However, in the old days widening spans of control was problematic because the culture in which it

Figure 5.6

DeBureaucratization: Increasing Span

RATIONALE:
Creating middle managers raises span issues

PROBLEM:
Trying to minimize levels and retain control
leads to staff proliferation
Too many managers produce narrow spans

ACTION:
Match Span to Layers with Staff Reduction
  *Workforce control increased
  Surveillance reduction
  Critical function responsibility
  Whole tasks, process understanding
  Team and self-determination*

TOOLS:
Role Negotiations
Staff Elimination

occurred emphasized control and oversight. It was harder to watch and check people with wider spans, but we still wanted the benefits of flatter organizations. The answer was to widen spans and flatten organizations, and then give managers staff units to help them watch people.

You may wonder why staff units spend so much time in other people's business, and so little time in actually producing something of value. The answer is simple: this is what they were created to do in the first place! If they were watching and checking, then managers could be free for managing. Watching and controlling replaces doing for many staff groups, and they do not really make much of a contribution as a consequence.

The solution is clear. Management spans should be widened by expanding the role of both managers and the workforce, as described in the previous sections. Widening spans by increasing

Figure 5.7
Debureaucratization: De-layering

RATIONALE:
Middle managers create hierarchy

PROBLEM:
Too many managers, incorrect
delegation create too many layers

ACTION:
Reduce layers

> Reduce layers
> Force delegation
> Raise control issues
> Reeducate middle managers
> Increase span

TOOLS:
Span reduction

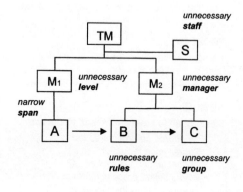

staff activities violates the method-as-model principle. It creates boundaries, decreases ownership, encourages politics, decreases initiative, fragments processes, discourages collaboration, and inhibits speed. It is the prevailing logic for increasing spans of control, and it is wrong.

De-layering

Increasing spans of control naturally delayers the organization. The preceding discussion makes it clear that wider spans should be based on empowering role expansions for both managers and the work-force, and not by adding additional staff to do our watching for us. This process is summarized in Figure 5.7.

In most de-layering, however, the number of levels is determined either indirectly by downsizing, or "by decree." This is because most of these efforts are cost-driven. Firms downsize to reduce costs.[12] Spans initially stay the same because there have been no adjustments in relative influence between managers and the workforce (the old Stage I or II logic has been retained, in which optimal spans were believed to be around six).[13] The number of layers in any organization is approximately determined by dividing the total number of positions by the average span of control. Dividing smaller size (from downsizing) by the same span of controls results in fewer layers. Alternatively, top management may simply decree that there will be a reduction in the number of layers following downsizing.

An undesirable result therefore looks desirable. Costs go down (in the short run) and the organization looks leaner and ready for the future. Nothing could be further from the truth. The organization has been "dumbsized," to borrow from one business writer.[14] The new structure is not process-driven. It has the wrong departments, and old irrelevant rules for coordinating them. Its spans of control are too narrow, encouraging micro-management and stifling individual contributions. We have ideally structured the firm for failure, and statistics show that we are getting it.

Summary of Actions for Debureaucratizing Structures

The debureaucratization model is the basic concept for reforming structures. The model has six highly interdependent elements: tasks, departmentation, rules, delegation, spans, and levels. Each element of the model has an associated action (critical change factor) and tool for debureaucratization. Basing tasks on process understanding is the first action. Reducing departmentation, eliminating rules, and expanding roles follow and are critical for producing a process-focused organi-

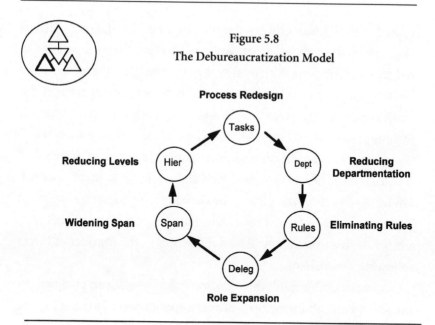

Figure 5.8
The Debureaucratization Model

Process Redesign

Reducing Levels · Hier · Tasks

Reducing Departmentation · Dept

Widening Span · Span

Eliminating Rules · Rules

Role Expansion · Deleg

Mistakes in Debureaucratization:

Misunderstanding the Logic of Debureaucratization
Misunderstanding the Rationale for Debureaucratization
Overdoing It
False Expectations

---

zation. Widening spans and de-layering are the final steps in debu-reaucratizing the firm and must not be undertaken without completing the first steps. The debureaucratization model, complete with the actions and tools for implementing it, is shown in Figure 5.8.

Mistakes in Debureaucratization

The sections above have discussed some of the important mistakes that are being made as firms attempt to restructure and reengineer themselves. This section briefly highlights these and summarizes several other problems that must be avoided in reforming structures. These mistakes are the following.

Misunderstanding the Rationale for Debureaucratization

The section on de-layering made it clear that debureaucratization ought to be based upon the idea of building organizational capability, and not upon cost reduction. I will not repeat these arguments here, except to say that disguising cost-driven downsizing and de-layering as empowerment and debureaucratization doesn't fool anyone.

Misunderstanding the Logic of Debureaucratization

This error is closely related to the first one. As the sections above have demonstrated, the decisions involved in creating the basic structure of an organization are highly interdependent. Manipulating any one element of the process (most often departments, spans, or layers) without accounting for the effects this will have on the others ensures an unfocused organization. For example, rules are created to coordinate tasks and departments. Manipulating departments without changing rules and procedures leaves us with a new set of departments and the old set of rules. Most of these rules are now irrelevant.

Similarly, de-layering without first adjusting spans means demoting managers without empowering the workforce and without giving them any voice in the process. The only way we can have fewer levels is to have fewer managers. Consider the following typical example of forming "self-managing work teams," shown in Figure 5.9. If we eliminate layer 2 in this structure, each level 3 manager would have 42 direct reports (the 36 members of the six workgroups and the six former managers) instead of 6. If we merge our six former managers into these workgroups, six managers are demoted and six workgroups are leaderless. We need a name for these leaderless groups and decide to call them self-managing work teams even though they have no idea of what self-managing means. All of the former level 2 managers will have been demoted. Each level 3 manager who was used

Figure 5.9
Misunderstanding the Logic of Debureaucratization

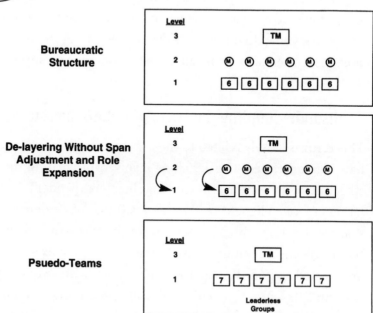

to managing six managers now leads six self-managing pseudo-teams, each of which has at least one disgruntled "member" (former leader). The potential of this working very well is not high.

Similar examples are possible for each organizing element in the model. All of these results are predictable from the debureaucratization logic developed above. In each case, an error results from changing one element of the model without considering the impact on other elements that are related to it.

Overdoing It

Debureaucratization does not mean no structure. That is explicitly *not* what I am arguing for in this chapter. Debureaucratization means building process-driven structures that accomplish critical goals with a minimum of rules and hierarchy, and that enable and encourage empowerment. Overdoing it means going too far. The performance model of Chapter 3 states that performance is the product of motivation, ability, and understanding. No one is able to do and understand everything, regardless of how motivated they are. Some structure is needed to focus task understanding and permit the development of expertise. Building organizations based upon capabilities generally means less structure, but certainly not eliminating it.

False Expectations

False expectations is in some ways a corollary of overdoing it. False expectations means that we expect the new organization to have none of the features of the older forms. A good case in point is matrix management. Some authors have enthusiastically predicted the death of matrix organizations. Complex organizations will not disappear, nor should they. The error is not in using complex forms, it is in using them prematurely. In the past organizations rushed to solve their problems structurally. Like all fads in management, we tended to overdo it.

The "Law of the Instrument"[15] is relevant here. It states: "Give a small boy a hammer, and he will find that everything needs pounding." In the past we used structure too much. Now we are "destructuring" too much. The problem is getting it right.

The ideas in this chapter are about getting it right. Basic structure should build upon people's capabilities and allow the full use and development of their potential. Structures and systems should enable empowerment and contribution, and they need to be transformed in the ways that we have discussed up to this point. However, these processes are not antithetical to complex forms. At some point, more horsepower will still be needed and we should not neglect the structural tools that we have developed to assist us. We will use them after the steps I have outlined in the preceding chapters and not before, but we are likely to need them nonetheless. This will require the sophisticated application of complex lateral forms in the context of Stage III organizations.[16]

The Price Waterhouse
Structural Transformation Project

It is now time to use these concepts to analyze a very important organizational transformation. I have chosen the Price Waterhouse Market Focused Organization project because it clearly illustrates the most important ideas of this chapter and provides a visible example of best practice in reforming structures, and because until this point the story has not been shared outside of Price Waterhouse.

Strategic Context for the Transformation

The structural transformation at Price Waterhouse began in 1993. At that time the U.S. economy was recovering from recession, and the future of the professional services industry was not clear. Price Waterhouse continued to outperform most of the other firms in its industry, but competition in its core markets had resulted in almost no increase in real share value since 1983. One of the causes of this stagnation was that audit fees had stalled, forcing all of the big accounting firms to seek growth in new client markets and services such as consulting. Four of the "Big Eight" firms had merged, forming two larger companies with significant economies of scale, critical mass in their key markets, and substantial resources in relation to their competitors. When these mergers were completed,

Price Waterhouse became the smallest of the remaining "Big Six" firms in terms of revenue, number of partners, and staff.

Technology was also changing rapidly. Firms were making major investments in an effort to improve efficiency and reduce costs. It did not seem likely that any one firm would establish a sustainable competitive advantage through technology, but it did seem clear that those who failed to invest would place themselves at a disadvantage. Price Waterhouse responded vigorously. By 1993 Price Waterhouse believed that it had more PCs per person than any of its competitors. Moreover, these systems were highly compatible throughout the United States. They had also become an early adopter of *Lotus Notes*—a tool that became the communications package leader during this time period. Other Price Waterhouse innovations included *PW Researcher* (a CD-ROM product), *Tax Workstation,* and *APEX 2.0* (for audit activities). These technological changes were altering the way the firm conducted its business and managed its relationships with its customers.

Price Waterhouse was also not immune to the changes in values that were discussed in Chapter 1. It was becoming more difficult to hire and retain the best graduates of top business schools. Turnover had always been high in professional services firms, but the costs of turnover, both financial and strategic, were becoming prohibitive. Work/family issues were more important than ever before. The personal costs of becoming a partner at a top professional services firm like Price Waterhouse were seen as more daunting than they had been in the past. The firm had traditionally led the industry in many human resource practices and in compensation, but by 1993 these benefits and programs were being matched by competitors.

In the face of these substantial changes in competition, technology, and values, and following a decision not to merge with Arthur Andersen, the firm had decided on a three-part strategy: first, to provide the highest-quality client services in the industry; second, to exercise "selectivity" in markets, clients, and services, thereby focusing their competencies on initiatives with maximum value to the firm; and third, to recruit, develop, and retain the "best and brightest" talent.

Interestingly, this strategy was not substantially different from that of the other top professional services firms. Arthur Andersen, Coopers & Lybrand, Deloitte and Touche, and Ernst and Young were all encountering similar industry conditions and had adopted similar strategies. Facing the same conditions and with a similar strategy, the firm's chairman and senior partner Shaun O'Malley believed that *strategy implementation would be the key to their success in the future.*

Reforming Structures at Price Waterhouse: Organizational Structure 1993

In 1993, Price Waterhouse was organized as shown in Figure 5.10. The structure that they operated in was a sophisticated and complex matrix organization with four major dimensions. Like most accounting firms their organization had a strong geographic focus inherited from the days when it was critical for partners to be geographically close to their clients in order to be responsive to their needs. Over the years, as the firm diversified and the services that they provided proliferated, a services dimension had been added to the structure. More recently, the demands of particular markets had required Price Waterhouse to focus on their particular needs. Because these markets crossed regional boundaries, they had been matrixed with the first two dimensions of the structure. Finally, clients had been segmented on the basis of size.

Operating such a complicated structure is challenging, but Price Waterhouse had been very successful in implementing its strategy

Figure 5.10

Matrix Structure

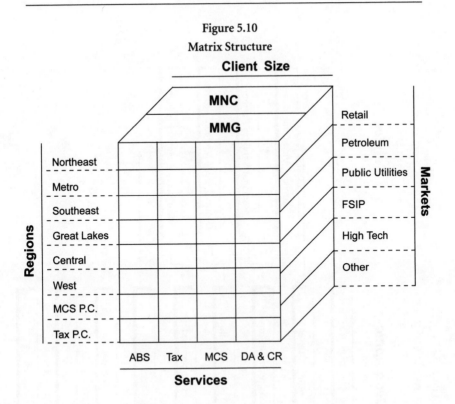

despite this complexity. However, they recognized that although a simple structure would likely never allow them to meet the simultaneous demands of markets, services, and geography, the complexity of their organization was inconsistent with what was to become their core competence—execution and effective strategy implementation.

Figure 5.11 illustrates operating relationships at the beginning of 1993. Partners reported directly to an Office Managing Partner but also had a solid-line relationship to an Office Service Managing Partner. They had a dotted-line relationship to a Regional Market Leader and a National Service Market Leader, who both reported informally to a National Market Leader. The structure violated

Figure 5.11
Market/Geographic/Service

Market   **Geographic**   **Service**

Chairman

Co-Chairmen Operations

Regional Vice Chairman

Group Managing Partner

Office Managing Partner

Partner

Manager

Senior

Staff

Services Vice Chairman

Regional Services Partner

Group Service Managing Partner

Office Service Managing Partner

National Market Leader

Regional Market Leader

National Service Market Leader

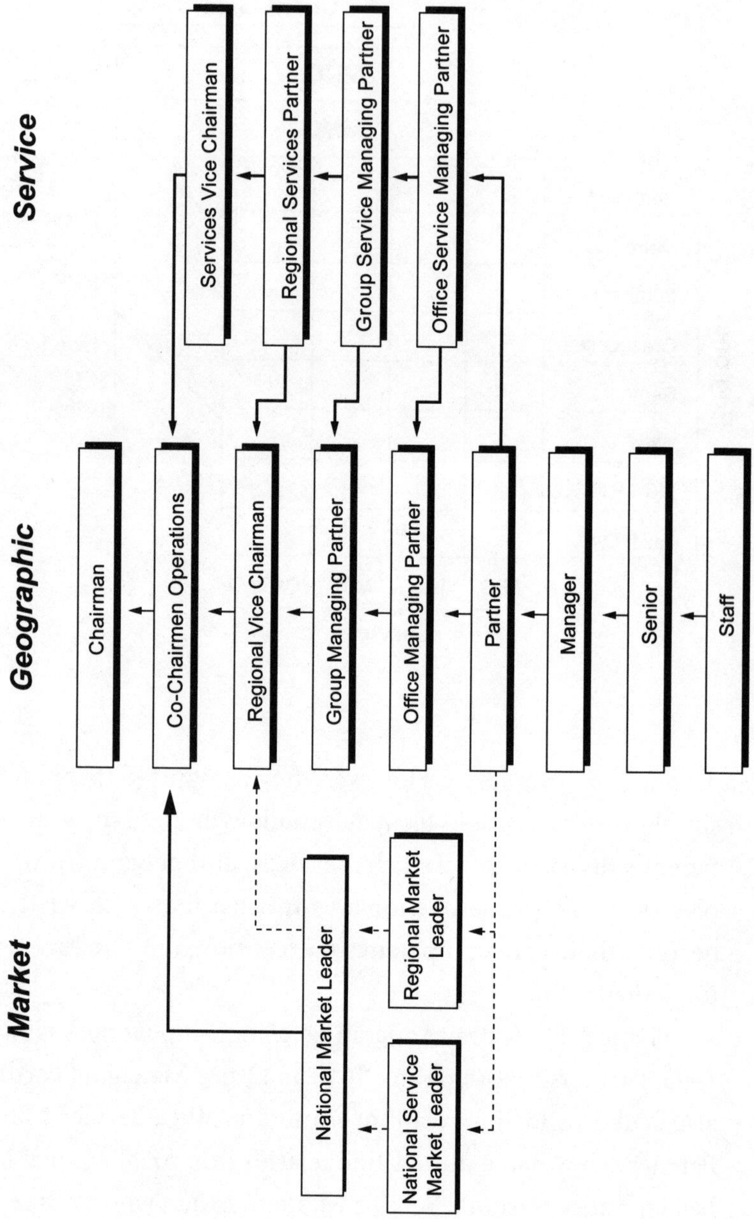

Figure 5.10

Matrix Structure

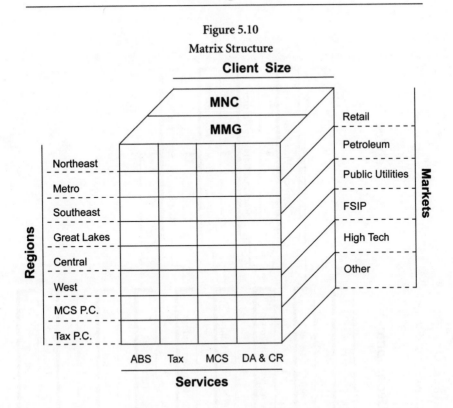

despite this complexity. However, they recognized that although a simple structure would likely never allow them to meet the simultaneous demands of markets, services, and geography, the complexity of their organization was inconsistent with what was to become their core competence—execution and effective strategy implementation.

Figure 5.11 illustrates operating relationships at the beginning of 1993. Partners reported directly to an Office Managing Partner but also had a solid-line relationship to an Office Service Managing Partner. They had a dotted-line relationship to a Regional Market Leader and a National Service Market Leader, who both reported informally to a National Market Leader. The structure violated

Figure 5.11
Market/Geographic/Service

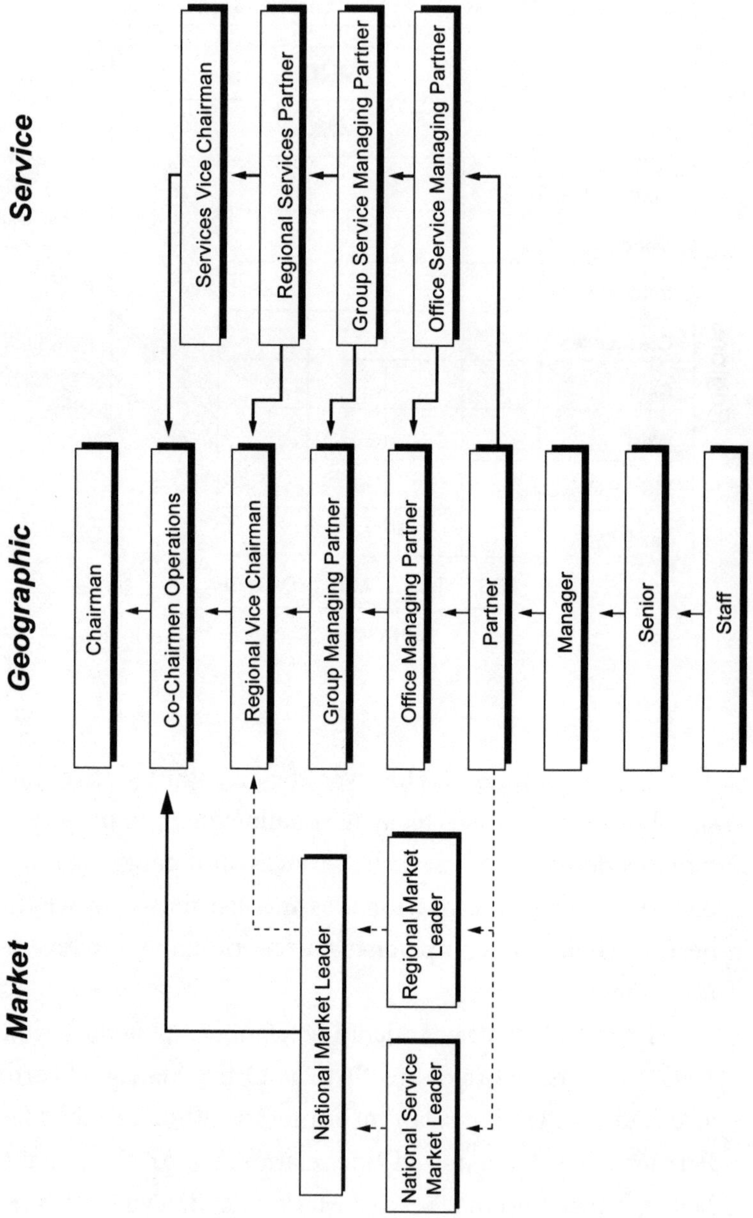

almost every traditional principle of management and was extremely complex even by matrix management standards, but it was delivering sustained high performance. The question was, could it deliver even more—enough to differentiate Price Waterhouse from the rest of the Big Six firms?

Debureaucratizing Price Waterhouse

Step 1: Identifying Core Processes

The first step in the debureaucratization model is to identify the core strategic processes of the firm. In recent years focusing on markets had been becoming more and more important to the operations of the firm. This was precisely the reason that a market focus had been added to the organization and become an additional dimension of the matrix. However, Figure 5.11 clearly shows the relative strength of this dimension in relation to both the services and geographic dimensions. Both services and geography had strong direct reporting lines from the bottom of the organization to the top. These dimensions were matrixed with one another but both had direct-line authority. The markets, however, had only a dotted-line relationship. Important sources of influence like control of profit-and-loss statements and performance appraisal responsibility remained in the geographic and service dimensions of the structure.

As markets gained in importance, geography was becoming less important than it had been in the past. Some of the services, like consulting, hardly had any geographic focus, and within others technology was moderating the need for close proximity that had once been paramount. Analysis of the geographic reporting structure indicated a hierarchical and perhaps overly bureaucratic layering on the geographic dimension of the matrix as shown in Figure 5.12.

Step 2: Reducing Departmentation through Process Focus

Price Waterhouse leadership realized that the matrix was overstructured on the geographic side and that the excessive layering was leading to slower than necessary decision making and narrow spans of control. Decision making needed to be accelerated to meet the goals of the transformation, and narrow spans were inconsistent with their strategy of hiring the best and the brightest. Few people of the caliber that they wished to attract wanted to work in such a controlling environment. The question was, could they afford to reduce departmentation and layers on the geographic side, particularly since it was this structure that had served the firm for so long and so well?

Focusing on processes yielded the answer. By increasing the importance of the market side of the matrix, increased coordination of the firm's many differentiated services could be obtained. Prior to an increase in the lateral focus on the core markets, this coordination had had to be achieved hierarchically, through the group levels of the geographic organization. By increasing the influence of the market side of the house, this coordination would be unnecessary and the structure could be de-layered, shortening the chain of command, increasing decision speed, and providing more emphasis on critical market activities. In this new form the strengthened market departments substituted for the geographic markets, reducing departmentation.

Step 3: Reducing Rules and Procedures

The debureaucratization model indicates that fewer departments require fewer rules and procedures for coordinating them. Figure 5.12 shows that one critical organizational procedure—the preparation and reporting of the profit-and-loss statement—was conducted at the office, group, regional, and national levels of the firm. This was a daunting task. With fewer departments, this task could be eliminated at the group level.

Figure 5.12
Current Regional P & L Structure

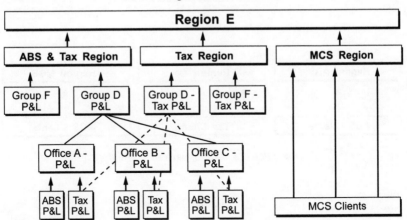

Step 4: Role Expansion

Managers at the office level no longer needed direct coordination from the groups due to the information being provided through the market side of the matrix. Consequently they were able to focus more on market issues while still maintaining required levels of geographic coordination. They began to become market, as well as geographic and services, experts. This role expansion was what allowed the firm to remove the group level from the geographic dimension of the matrix. It was no longer needed.

Step 5: De-layering and Span Adjustment

The consequence of the preceding steps was that the geographic organization was de-layered as shown in Figure 5.13 (for the services side of the organization). The final structure is shown in Figure 5.14. Price Waterhouse feels that as a consequence of the transformation it has accomplished a number of objectives. I have summarized their appraisal, along with the relationship of their objectives to the adaptive culture dimensions, below.

Figure 5.13
Proposed Regional Discipline P & L Structure

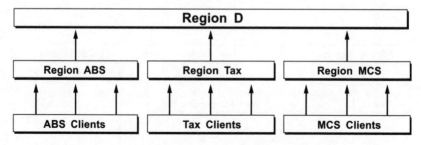

Discipline P&Ls–Summarized at Region

Figure 5.14
Proposed Structure
Service/Market Focus Within Existing Regions

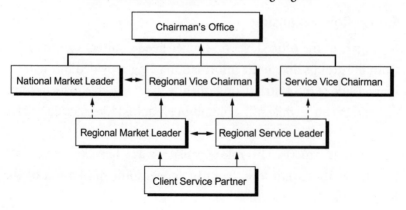

Table 5.1

Price Waterhouse Evaluation	Adaptive Culture Dimension
The organization is more externally focused	*External focus*
Market focus is increased	*Process focus, ownership*
The reporting structure is simplified	*Speed*
The reporting structure is flatter	*Boundaryless*
Individual partners are empowered	*Ownership*

Summary

Reforming structures goes beyond restructuring and reengineering to accomplish a fundamental "reformation" of the basic structure of the firm. The basic concept for reforming structures is the debureaucratization model. The model states that foundation tasks drive decisions about departmentation, rules, delegation, spans, and layers. These decisions are highly interdependent. Each solves a problem posed by the decision coming before it, but then raises a new one. Forming departments answers the question of who should do what tasks, but raises the question of how these departments should be coordinated. Rules are established to coordinate departments, but then raise the question of how exceptions to rules should be managed, and so on.

Each action (critical change factor) for reforming structures answers one of these questions as shown in Figure 5.8. The specific actions that implement debureaucratization are *reducing departmentation, eliminating rules, expanding roles, increasing spans,* and *delayering.* Each of these has an associated tool, such as the RAMMP matrix or role negotiations.

The concepts, actions, and tools for reforming structures must meet a stringent set of criteria. First, they must *support* the strategy of the firm. Second, they must be consistent with and *enable* earlier steps in the change process. This is accomplished by defining the basic tasks of the firm in terms of its core strategic processes. These processes were identified and designed in the engaging systems stage of *MegaChange,* and are directly based on the firm's strategic objectives. Basing structure on strategic processes builds a process orientation into the fundamental structure of the firm, ensures that this structure supports critical strategic objectives, and supports earlier changes at the engaging systems step of *MegaChange.* Finally, the new structure must *model* and extend the desired future culture. The actions and tools for implementing the debureaucratization model directly model the adaptive culture.

The debureaucratization model helps us to understand why so many downsizing and de-layering efforts fail. Four common mistakes explain these failures. They are misunderstanding the rationale of debureaucratization, misunderstanding its logic, overdoing it, and establishing false expectations for the change effort. These mistakes can be avoided by using the concepts, actions, and tools presented in this chapter.

The Price Waterhouse structural transformation project provides a clear illustration of the debureaucratization model and how its use can allow us to avoid the major mistakes in reforming structures. It also illustrates the applicability of the model in highly complex strategic situations, as well as in simpler ones. Debureaucratization does not mean no structure; it means the *right amount* of structure. Too little can be as bad as too much.

Reforming structures raises new issues for management, just as the steps for engaging systems and empowering the workforce did. Empowerment required changes in human resource systems. Systems changes required changes in structure to support new strategic processes. Reforming structures also raises new challenges that must be addressed at the next step of *MegaChange.*

Three of these "dilemmas" are as follows. Most people define success on the basis of moving up in the organization. In the future there will be fewer layers of hierarchy. How will we motivate people in de-layered organizations? Role expansion widens spans and limits the possibilities of micro-management. This facilitates the adaptive culture, but raises the issues of how firms can maintain control without oversight. Finally, debureaucratization means less access to traditional means of coordination. Culture must replace rules and hierarchy for this purpose. New systems support the new culture, as discussed at the end of Chapter 4, but they are not enough. The final step in the *MegaChange* process, *redirecting strategy*, addresses these concerns from a strategic perspective. There is much to be learned here, and it is to these issues that I now turn.

Remaking Strategy

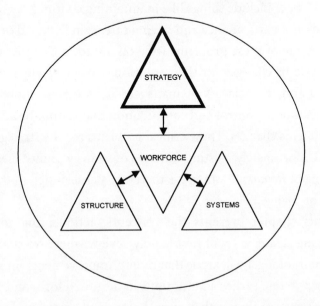

I began my discussion of the steps in *MegaChange* with a summary of the strategic actions that top management must take to create awareness and legitimation for future change activities. In this chapter I return to the concept of strategy and its importance in transforming organizations, but at a much higher level. Whereas before I stated that strategies must signal and support the need for change, I now argue that strategy must move beyond creating awareness and legitimation and be radically transformed and redirected.

The strategy concept is unnecessarily impoverished, and fails to deliver on its potential. This is because strategic concepts—like our structures, systems, and views of the workforce—are mired in Stage I and II thinking. Recent "breakthroughs" in strategy do little to improve things; they simply embrace the old ways of thinking, with new language and minor modifications.

Reaching a higher standard of performance requires completing all the steps in *MegaChange* described up until this point. But along the way, creating new structures and systems poses some new challenges. These include things like maintaining contingency between rewards and performance and having careers in flattened organizations. Some of these problems were discussed in Chapter 4, along with systems changes for their solution. However, wider spans of control and fewer layers of management also raise fundamental concerns about control and coordination that cannot be addressed with systems changes. These critical problems require strategic solutions. Unfortunately, existing concepts of strategy cannot meet these challenges. *Remaking strategy* is therefore a crucial step in the latter stages of change.

This chapter presents the concepts, actions, and tools for remaking strategy. I will first briefly review where we stand with current thinking. I will argue that recent "improvements" in strategy simply reiterate earlier assumptions in disguised form and perpetuate the very problems they were designed to eliminate. I will also show that even when new ideas like "core competence," strategic intent," and "strategy formation" are implemented successfully, they are still inadequate. Following this I will present the criteria for remaking strategy. I will then propose a solution to these dilemmas and challenges.

This discussion will introduce the two major concepts of this chapter: "shared meaning" and "mutually recognized interdependence." These concepts have an extensive research background that is generally unknown in the strategy literature, and that is vital for reforming the concept. The last sections of the chapter present the actions and tools for remaking strategy, and lead us to the final, third portion of the book.

Strategy: The Old Way

The first two stages of organization, bureaucracy (Stage I) and complex organizations (Stage II), each have corresponding strategic concepts. To a very large extent the strategic assumptions and methods used within these stages are consistent with the corresponding models of organization. Strategy and structure both tended to follow from the prevailing nature of the competitive situation and from similar assumptions about human behavior.

Stage I: Strategic Planning and Strategy Formulation

Early bureaucratic organizations made use of very simple planning processes. One of the first forms of "strategy" was what is now known as extrapolative planning.[1] Strategy was nothing more than rudimentary budgeting, where what we would do next year was determined as a simple multiple of what we did last year. The adequacy of extrapolative planning diminished as business environments became more complex, and extrapolative planning was replaced by processes for "strategy formulation." Whereas extrapolative planning was almost exclusively inwardly focused, strategy formulation looked outside the organization and attempted to determine desirable courses of action based on threats and opportunities in the environment and the firm's strengths and weaknesses. This was the beginning of "competitive strategy."[2]

In bureaucratic (Stage I) organizations strategy formulation activities became vested in the hands of top management and professional planning staffs. Strategies were formulated by "planners" and communicated to "doers" in a manner that denied the legitimate contributions that could, and should, be made by the workforce. Frustrated by plans that seemed out of touch with business and technical realities, the workforce often ignored the firm's formal plans.

I clearly remember a consulting engagement in which I was asked to evaluate a prominent firm's strategic planning processes. I asked to see the strategy that had been produced by their planning group. The documents that I received were extensive and included virtually every "tool" then being promulgated by every major strategic consulting firm and also within academe. Yet no one really used any of it! When I asked why not, the business leader said that they only participated in the strategic planning process to keep the planning staff happy. They had even assigned one person full time to handle data gathering and liaison with the corporate planning staff. They managed their business—one that had been in the original *In Search of Excellence* study by Peters and Waterman[3] and that was remarkably successful—on the basis of a three-page plan they had developed *themselves.*

Strategy formulation presumed the omniscience of top managers, planning staffs, and consultants and denied the legitimate and necessary contributions of others throughout the organization. Formulation was born out of the necessity of responding to complex business conditions and higher rates of change than extrapolative planning could cope with. It became necessary to anticipate and plan for these changes. However, by concentrating responsibility for these activities exclusively in the hands of top management and planners, strategies became dominated by information that was often unrealistic, too formalized, and not current enough. The pace of competitive change quickly outdistanced the capabilities of these processes. Organizations began to transition to Stage II—complex organization forms. Along with this came a new paradigm of strategic thinking.

Stage II: Strategy Formation

The planning practices of many firms are still mired in the Stage I thinking outlined above. However, these too-simple concepts of formulation have begun to be replaced by a newer way of thinking about strategy called "strategy formation." This new concept is more sophisticated than the formulation idea and addresses some of its limitations.

Strategy formation is the name given to the process for "forming" strategy in a complicated organizational (as opposed to individual) decision-making process. In this approach the top manager is not the creator of the strategy, but rather the orchestrator of the process through which the strategy is formed. This method of strategic decision making was identified by Charles Lindblom in studies of political decision making,[4] was incorporated into business strategy practice by James Brian Quinn,[5] and was introduced into business education in a book by Quinn and Henry Mintzberg.[6] Extensive research in organizational decision making[7,8,9] supports the fact that many important strategic decisions are made according to the processes described in the model.

The strategy formation concept acknowledges the decision-making limitations of top managers and planning staffs. Rather than proposing that strategy can be successfully "formulated" by these groups, strategy formation concepts embrace a "messier" incremental process in which the inputs and contributions of a wider set of participants are solicited and included, yielding a more relevant and politically acceptable strategy.

Strategy formation processes are observed in organizations in which there are multiple groups concerned with strategy development—divisions and headquarters, line and staff, projects and programs, and multiple functional groups—in short, in Stage II: complex organizations. In such organizations simple top-down formulation processes do not work because of the complexity of the situation and the need for all the affected groups to support the strategy.

In its simplest form, the strategy formation process has four steps and extends over a long period, often as long as 10 years.

These steps are called the *awareness, information, consensus,* and *commitment* stages of forming the strategy.[10] Awareness refers to a period in which members of the organization began to appreciate the need for change. The information stage is a step in which information is systematically introduced into the emerging decision process from multiple, and often competing, sources. This information is then crystallized and focused in the consensus stage. Finally, after the three previous steps in the process have been accomplished, a public commitment is made to a decision which, in effect, has already been made as a consequence of the three preceding stages.

Strategy formation is a definite improvement on earlier thinking. It recognizes the need for more involvement in strategic decision making within the organization. It also recognizes the very real behavioral limits that encumber large-scale change. People resist change not only because they cannot understand it but also because they cannot accept it. Strategy formation processes address the complexity of the competitive and organizational setting, and do not make the same simplistic assumptions about executive omniscience that were made by the formulation model.

On the surface, everything is well. However, hidden within the formation perspective is a set of assumptions that will not let it be extended to Stage III organizations and hypercompetitive environments. The inadequacy of Stage I and II practices requires new strategic thinking for the future.

Remaking Strategy: The Failure of Strategy Formulation and Formation

Stage I (formulation) and Stage II (formation) thinking about strategy are inadequate for two reasons. First, both formulation and formation ideas share an incorrect set of assumptions about human behavior in organizations. Second, even though formation concepts improve upon earlier concepts, they are inadequate for addressing the challenges inherent in moving to Stage III conditions of hypercompetition and change.

What's New Is Really Old

Formation concepts are often offered as the new alternative to older formulation ideas. However, these ideas have far more in common than meets the eye, and what they share is dangerous and incorrect. On the surface strategy formation ideas seem to avoid the negative assumptions made in formulation models. But we only have to scratch the surface to see that this avoidance is more apparent than real. Two simple questions reveal the similarity of the assumptions made in both approaches. First, whose goals are being advanced by the strategy? And, second, how were these goals arrived at?

For formulation, it is clear that the goals that are being implemented are those of management. Formation ideas disguise this fact. Management realizes that inputs from the workforce are necessary, and manipulates lower levels to extract what *it* wants. While its vision may be changing, it is still *management's* vision. Without legitimate participation, the content of strategy remains in the hands of managers. As Victor Thompson notes: "Since neither the official values nor the product of most organizations can be very important to most of the people in them [due to a lack of participation] acceptance of goals must be obtained by manipulation."[11] And it is.

Formulation and formation activities violate the method-as-model principle. Managers navigate "corridors of indifference"[12] to advance their causes with the least opposition, publicly ask for commitment only after the decision has already been made, and structure decision-making processes so that only one—their preferred—solution can emerge. There can be little doubt that these processes allow managers to produce and guide decisions with an unseen hand; that the final outcome remains firmly in their grasp is incontrovertible. The specific techniques advocated by formation processes make this point over and over again. Formulation and formation therefore do not differ at all in this respect, except that formulation processes make their procedures public.

Formulation and formation processes cannot advance the adaptive culture because their methods embody the very antithesis of empowerment, engagement, and capability. Their actions assert their belief that only management can lead, that management's objectives are paramount, and that people should get out of the way and not resist management's programs. Nothing could be further from the truth at this point in time. Formation and formulation are impoverished notions, either denying human capabilities or using them illegitimately, thereby ensuring that they will never be realized to their full extent. It is time for a change.

Stage I and II Strategy Concepts Fail to Resolve Critical Challenges

The section above indicated that formulation and formation concepts make unacceptable assumptions about human behavior and capabilities, and as a consequence result in practices that model precisely the wrong culture for the future. In this section I will argue that these ideas fail not only on these grounds, but also because they are inadequate for resolving the strategic challenges inherent in future organizations.

Strategy—whether at Stage I, II, or III of evolution—must always perform three critical functions. These are the *directional, motivational,* and *coordinative* functions of strategy. Strategy sets an

intended future direction for the firm, motivates participation in achieving it, and coordinates activities along the way. Other elements of the *MegaChange* model, in particular systems and structures, also must support these objectives. Since systems, strategies, and structures must be mutually reinforcing, consistent, and synergistic, it is generally the case that elements from one stage of organization (bureaucratic, complex, or adaptive) cannot be mixed with those from another.

This is especially true when we reach Stage III organization forms. Stage I and II formulation and formation activities are *not* consistent with Stage III approaches to systems and structures. For example, Stage III organizations utilize less hierarchy than earlier bureaucratic or complex forms. Consequently, Stage I and II formulation and formation processes are ineffective because they *require* hierarchy for control, direction, and motivation—the three critical functions for any strategy. This fact raises three challenges or "dilemmas" for strategy at Stage III. These challenges, cast in terms of the critical functions required of any strategy as presented above, are achieving motivation without promotions, control without oversight, and coordination without hierarchy.

The dilemmas arise from earlier steps in the change process—in empowering the workforce, engaging systems, and especially in reforming structures. It is in these steps that we reduce oversight and hierarchy, both of which are critical to traditional means of control, coordination, and motivation, as noted above. However, we do not want to undo any of the actions that we have taken because each is an essential step—a critical change factor—in creating more productive, capable, and satisfying organizations.

And so, we encounter the dilemmas. De-layering removes obstacles to empowerment, but raises issues about coordination. Wider spans eliminate excessive checking and micro-management, but raise issues about how control can be maintained without detailed knowledge of each individual's performance. Fewer managers means fewer positions to aspire to for promotion. In this new transformed context, strategy must provide the necessary direction, motivation, and coordination, but traditional methods of formulation and formation are too weak for this purpose.

Why are formation and formulation concepts so inadequate? They are not motivational because the goals they produce are of little interest to anyone other than the managers who politically installed them. True coordination and cooperation, in the sense that my colleague Lawrence Hrebiniak uses the term,[13] is not possible because both formulation and formation focus primarily on overcoming resistance rather than on encouraging collaboration. Cooperation presumes the desire to be coordinated,[14] which is absent if the only agreement is simply not to resist. Not resisting is hardly equivalent to proactive cooperation.

Finally, all control in Stage I and II strategy is manipulative. Manipulation requires manipulators, and hence is impossible in situations where managerial oversight no longer exists. Strategy formulation and formation processes are therefore completely inadequate for resolving the dilemmas of motivation without promotions, coordination without hierarchy, and control without oversight. We should stop wasting our time on them.

Remaking Strategy: Criteria

The criteria for remaking strategy follow directly from the deficiencies of Stage I and II strategic thinking outlined above. Remaking strategy requires concepts that provide direction, motivation, and coordination, and particularly resolve the dilemmas of motivation without promotions, control without oversight, and coordination without hierarchy.

Meeting the criteria poses a real challenge. Years of effort have yielded inadequate concepts of formation and formulation that obstruct rather than further opportunities for real change in strategy. Yet the review and criteria above do show the direction for change. The central theme of these criticisms is also the central theme of this book. We must base our organizations on human capabilities rather than limitations, and allow these capabilities to be applied to the determination of the purposes of the organization. The shared sense of mission and vision that results must embody a culture that allows for the productive engagement of these capabilities and aspirations in the accomplishment of meaningful work. In remaking strategy, we must conduct ourselves in a way that does not compromise these higher standards. In short, we must make our organizations—their systems, strategies, and structures—more human.

So far we have failed at this at the strategic level. Mired in regressive thinking, impoverished assumptions, and old models of organization, strategy practice takes place in an environment manifestly unfit for it. This failure has been less visible than the disastrous attempts at downsizing and de-layering only because we have come to expect less and less from strategy.

In the next sections I outline the two core concepts of this chapter, "shared meaning" and "mutually recognized interdependence," and show how implementing these concepts allows us to meet the criteria presented above. In doing so we come full circle in the stages of change, back to our original starting point—to the capability assumption and the higher standard—and to strategy, the starting and finishing point in the process of *MegaChange.*

Stage III: Concepts for Remaking Strategy

In this section I will develop the two core concepts and show how they go beyond earlier methods for addressing the directional, motivational, and coordinative functions of strategy. To understand the power of these concepts it is necessary to contrast them with the means utilized by Stage I and II approaches for these purposes.

Both shared meaning and mutually recognized interdependence build upon fundamental ideas concerning what makes anything "meaningful." They are both, therefore, directly related to the capability assumption and the higher standard concepts from Chapter 1. I shall argue that shared meaning is fundamentally a way of meeting the *directional* and *motivational* requirements for Stage III strategy, and that mutually recognized interdependence is the way for addressing the *coordinative* function. These ideas are related to, but are much more fundamental and powerful than, concepts of goals and goal consistency used for these purposes in formulation and formation models.

Remaking Strategy: Contrasts with Formulation and Formation Methods

The mechanisms used for obtaining direction, motivation, and coordination in Stage I and II organizations are summarized in Table 6.1. In bureaucratic (Stage I) organizations, direction was obtained through the imposition of *unilateral goals.* As I have discussed at length above, these goals were created by management with little input from the workforce. They served as standards for control and as the basis for rewards. Consistency was achieved through centralized planning, and by assigning goals to parts of the organization and then holding each part accountable for achieving them. In this sense, coordination was achieved by imposing a *legislated consistency* among goals.

In Stage II, centralized planning became impossible due to the complexity of the business environment and an increasing pace of change. Formation processes were created (ostensibly) to accommodate the interests of multiple stakeholders, along with those of management. The discussion in the first portions of this chapter indicates that this attempt at accommodation was more apparent than real: multiple stakeholders were allowed "voice" only to obtain their ideas for advancing management's, as opposed to their own, purposes.

Despite this limitation, formation processes *are* more participative than formulation processes, even if they are just as manipulative. Direction and motivation were obtained from a set of *shared goals*, as shown in Table 6.1. Shared goals emphasized building a common understanding of the actions that would be taken by each unit in the organization. These goals were at least partially the outcome of a process of bargaining and negotiation, a process always guided by the unseen hand of management. The direction that was set included the inputs of others, even if it was constantly circumscribed by an exclusively managerial agenda.

Motivationally, strategy formation recognized the so-called process limits of change.[15] In essence, formation processes were a way of avoiding resistance, even if it had to be done surreptitiously. As I have noted, this approach violated the method-as-model principle in this regard. However, formation processes did address the resistance to change that was caused by Stage I formulation processes and the unilateral imposition of goals.

Negotiation of shared goals allowed for better consistency among them. Because of the complexity and turbulence of business settings,

Table 6.1
Mechanisms for Obtaining Motivation, Direction, and
Control in Various Stages of Organization

Stage of Organization	Functions of Strategy		
	Motivation	Direction	Coordination
Stage I *Bureaucratic*	Direction	Unilateral goals	Legislated consistency
Stage II *Complex*	Overcome resistance	Shared goals	Negotiated consistency
Stage III *Adaptive*	Meaningful work	Shared meaning	Mutually recognized interdependence

legislated or planned consistency was imperfect; negotiation improved on this by accommodating local interests and information that was unknown to upper management and centralized planning staffs. However, true collaboration was rare. Although shared goals and a negotiated consistency among them helped by overcoming resistance, it was not the same as engendering commitment. Simply not resisting something falls far short of proactive collaboration and commitment.

Direction, motivation, and coordination were achieved in Stage I and II organizations through the management of goals and the consistency among them. Goals were initially unilateral and planned, and then negotiated and guided. Although progress was made, the concepts did not ensure that the goals were meaningful, or that they went beyond simple consistency to encourage true collaboration.

In Stage III, shared meaning replaces shared goals, and mutually recognized interdependence replaces negotiated consistency for achieving direction, motivation, and coordination. These concepts are based on fundamental research concerning meaning and motivation[16,17] and consensus as a mechanism for achieving coordination.[18]

Shared Meaning and Mutually Recognized Interdependence

The limitations of Stage I and II methods for achieving direction, motivation, and coordination are obvious from the discussion above. In fact, most of this chapter has been a critique of what is wrong with current strategic thinking. After having said what is wrong, it is now time to say what needs to be done for remaking strategy.

We can draw three conclusions from the discussion in the preceding section. First, goals are central to achieving direction and motivation at all stages of strategic development. Second, the extent to which these are shared and consistent facilitates coordination. Finally, although they were on the right track, formulation and formation methods did not go far enough. After correctly identifying goals and goal consistency as important steps in achieving direction, motivation, and coordination, strategic management researchers and practitioners never bothered to ask why these mechanisms worked. Stopped short by partial success, these approaches delivered on only a portion of their true potential.

What did these approaches miss? They failed to understand that the concept of *meaning* is what makes goals motivational and directional, and that the concept of *consensus* is what facilitates coordination. Shared goals and negotiated consistency are steps in the right direction, but they are weak in comparison to what is possible.

Shared Meaning

Shared meaning goes beyond shared goals by creating a purpose that not only is shared by all organization participants but also is *meaningful* to them. You and I may share the goal of increasing earnings per share as a condition of our employment, but if I don't really care about it—*if it is not meaningful to me*—I will exert less effort toward its accomplishment.

Most goals in organizations are so distant from human purposes and so aligned with management (as opposed to workforce) aspirations that they are almost meaningless to all but the highest levels of the firm. And these levels of the organization do not do the work! As I have said before, I do not believe that people get up in the morning to make earnings per share. They get up to make a product, to utilize skills that they are proud of, and to take care of their families. These are *meaningful* goals. Organizations can utilize this concept by creating shared meaning in strategy, and we will achieve unprecedented levels of satisfaction and productivity as a consequence.

An example may be useful here. I remember being at General Electric's AstroSpace division on the day that a particular spacecraft made the planetary fly-by that it had been designed for. The spacecraft satellite had been built by GE, and on that day some of the early photographs from the mission were being relayed to Astro-Space from the Jet Propulsion Laboratory in California. The excitement in AstroSpace was everywhere. I don't believe that people were excited because they thought that the stock price would rise, or that they might generate more earnings per share. They were excited because they had done something no one else had ever done before—built a spacecraft that obtained the first detailed photographs of the surface of Venus. This was far more powerful and motivational than achieving financial objectives.

Meaningful work is its own reward, and the motivation to be derived from it does not depend upon advancement through an artificial hierarchy in which there are 20 losers for every winner, by definition.[19] Internalized commitment to a purpose that is shared with others directs activity without the necessity of "watchers" and "checkers" monitoring performance and destroying motivation in the process. Shared meaning resolves the dilemmas of motivation without promotions and control without oversight by providing new, more powerful mechanisms for achieving direction and motivation that do not require hierarchy.

Mutually Recognized Interdependence

Consensus is a far more powerful concept than a negotiated consistency among goals. Think for a minute about why the two varieties of goal consistency that I have discussed facilitate coordination. Legislated consistency (Stage I) just means that your actions will fit with mine. It is not the case that I am necessarily aware of what you are trying to do. Consequently, I pursue my own goals without reference to your activities. When something changes, I continue to do the same thing until someone tells me to do differently. Adjustment therefore depends on management's ability to see the need for change, re-plan, and communicate new consistent goals for everyone. Obviously this cannot work in any but the simplest of situations.

Negotiated consistency (Stage II) improves on this by obtaining the consistency from negotiations among the affected parties. Each must have at least some understanding of the other in order to negotiate the goals. This allows for some adaptation when the situation changes. However, the negotiation is conducted from the perspectives of the affected parties, *guided by the unseen hand of management.* The purpose of the effort is therefore always fragmented and its context is obscure. Since management never overtly discloses its intentions, it becomes impossible to take these into account when adjustment is necessary. The initial negotiated consistency is management-guided, and subsequent adjustment is workforce-driven, simply because management purposes were never made plain at the outset.

The negotiation methods used in Stage II rely on bargaining, compromise, and the covert use of coercion. There is no real use of collaboration because, by definition, collaboration involves seeking a solution in which *all of the interests of all of the parties* are accommodated. Management guides the process but keeps its agenda secret. Without a clear management agenda there is little possibility of negotiating a win-win as opposed to win-lose solution, and most of the time it is the workforce that loses. Thus there can be little chance of shared meaning, and the negotiation at best can only produce consistency with respect to management's hidden goals.

Mutually recognized interdependence is based upon a stronger notion of consensus in which each person, group, and administrator is aware of their interdependence with one another for achieving shared meaning. We *recognize* the intentions of others and our *interdependence* with them for achieving our common, *mutual* purposes. There is therefore a consensus, not only among various work groups, but also among these groups and management, unlike the negotiated consistency in Stage II.

Consensus means not only that our local goals and actions are consistent with one another, but also that "I know that you know"[20] my intentions. Sharing and awareness of our mutual intentions facilitates adaptation and coordination because knowing what you intend to do is far more powerful than knowing what actions you are planning to take. Consensus about "why" is far more revealing than consensus about "what." With knowledge of why, I can accommodate changes far more effectively than I can when I have to guess what you are really trying to do from your actions.

Consensus means that we have reached a solution that we can all actively support, using a process in which the interests of all have been considered. It is much more likely that this will be a true win-win solution. Mutually recognized interdependence solves the coordination-without-hierarchy dilemma because it allows us to coordinate our activities based on a common understanding of our purposes and intentions. If I know what you intend to do, and if I share a common purpose with you, then it is not necessary to have a formal, hierarchical position to ensure coordination. Furthermore, since cooperation is motivated by shared meaning, it is proactive and collaborative in nature.

Actions for Remaking Strategy:
Building Shared Meaning and Mutually Recognized Interdependence

Building shared meaning and mutually recognized interdependence requires specific actions and tools. The next section presents the critical change factors for remaking strategy. The final section of the chapter will then present specific tools for implementing these actions.

Building Shared Meaning

There are three critical actions for building shared meaning. These are: *achieving through collaboration, humanizing the vision,* and *realizing hidden meaning.* All three actions are based on the concept of meaning developed in Chapter 1 when discussing the higher standard.

Achieving through Collaboration

An action is meaningful when it allows us to produce an effect on something. This basic aspect of meaning underlies much of the psychological research concerning job design and motivation. A large body of competently executed research shows that motivation increases when individuals perform work that allows accomplishment and achievement,[21] that lets workers perform "whole" tasks (and not just small specialized pieces) that impact on others, and that provides feedback that verifies the effects.[22] These are simply various ways in which individuals experience meaning by producing an effect on their work or on others.

It follows from this that something is more or less meaningful the greater or lesser extent to which it allows us to verify that something of importance has really been accomplished. The bigger the effect, the greater the meaning. Individual jobs give us a chance to experience meaning at an individual level, but what makes a strategy meaningful? Achieving through collaboration means accomplishing something that an individual could never hope to accomplish alone, and extends the meaning concept to the strategic level. The GE AstroSpace example illustrates this perfectly. No one person could have constructed the satellite, planned its mission, designed its telemetry, and placed it into orbit alone. Only collaboration made this possible. This collaboration made possible an achievement far beyond any individual's reach and produced a level of shared meaning that galvanized an entire organization.

Humanizing the Vision

Most of the critique in this chapter has been aimed at the failure of most strategies to provide any content that is meaningful to the workforce. Deriving meaning by accomplishing something requires not only that something happens as a consequence of our action but also that the something is of concern to us. It has to be an effect that we care about, one that is relevant to us in the sense of affecting our outcome and reflecting our values. A vision that contains abstract, nonhuman purposes that are really someone else's can hardly hope to achieve this outcome. Yet that is precisely what characterizes the content of most strategies. The official goals of the company are overly financial and nonhuman, and espouse the aspirations of management to the exclusion of those of the workforce. It's not surprising that they don't put much of a zing in our step.

At the individual level, we have learned that goal setting must include at least some personal goals in order to be motivational.[23] Yet when we extend goals from the individual level to the strategic level, this concept is lost, for the most part. To be sure, mission and vision statements routinely include pro forma and token acknowledgment of the need for "delegation" (and, more recently, "empowerment"), but one is hard pressed to identify the empowering processes that led to these ideas being included in the strategy in the first place. While most workers may want these things, it is more of a guess than a determination that they are important. Obviously, this violates the method-as-model principle, even if it does occasionally yield the proper content. Humanizing the content of strategy means including goals that are not exclusively financial and that represent the purposes of all participants in the organization, not simply a best guess derived from a misplaced sense of noblesse oblige. Humanizing the content of strategy means including more humans in the process of determining it.

Realizing Hidden Meaning

There seems to be an almost universal belief that most mission and vision statements are meaningless instead of meaningful. This is something of a paradox, however. If this is the case, why does almost every organization have one? Why are so many resources spent on developing them?

The answer can be found in a simple observation. Mission

statements are far more meaningful to the people who developed them than they are to the people they are communicated to. Part of this may be due to problems discussed under "Humanizing the Vision" above. However, I think that there is a more interesting possibility.

A mission, vision, or strategy has a hidden meaning that is not apparent from its content. This meaning is accessible only by those who were participants in creating it. Strategies, missions, and visions are usually created through a process involving intense discussion and exchange of ideas—we cannot fault senior management for not trying in this regard. In this process deep understandings are developed about what particular words or concepts in the mission mean—understandings that cannot be easily transmitted in a short, verbal mission "statement". Mission statements are constrained by attempts at brevity and pressures to imitate "managerially correct" thinking (Empowerment, Core Competence, Total Quality Management, Reengineering, etc.). Mission statements often become nothing more than the stringing together of managerially correct language and vague statements alluding to more important concepts in cryptic terms. For those who were in the room when the document was crafted these words have meaning. For those who were not part of the discussion they are platitudes like "motherhood" and "apple pie."

I believe that it is the *process* of developing the mission that makes it meaningful. Without participation, there can be little inclusion of workforce goals as advocated in "Humanizing the Vision" above. Without participation, the rich discussion of values, purposes, and aspirations that characterize the creation of a vision and that give it meaning will be understood only by those who were part of the dialogue and not by the people who are expected to embrace and enact them. Realizing hidden meaning means including more people in the process of creating the vision. The process, in this case, is just as important as the content.

Building Mutually Recognized Interdependence: Shared Intentions

Building mutually recognized interdependence implies first having created a sense of shared meaning or purpose. This is so because people become interdependent with respect to their purposes: they must collaborate in pursuit of shared objectives. With a sense of shared purpose it is then necessary to understand the process through which the organization intends to accomplish its objectives. This process "maps" the interdependence. When all parties understand this process and recognize their intentions and those of others in it— *when it is mutually recognized*—this understanding forms the basis for true collaboration and cooperation.

The actions for creating shared meaning are therefore prerequisite for building mutually recognized interdependence. In addition, it is necessary for everyone to understand their own intentions and the intentions of others in the process for obtaining it. On the surface, this sounds similar to the kind of "process mapping" performed as part of reengineering efforts, but it is really quite different. The mapping advocated here communicates what people *intend* to do, not abstract and inflexible steps in a "process without people." Ensuring that this process is shared completes the steps for building mutually recognized interdependence.

Mutually recognized interdependence builds upon fundamental concepts of meaning and consensus for remaking strategy. The concept of *shared intentions* is extremely important in this perspective. Shared intentions allow us to anticipate problems, act with greater speed, and collaborate in ways that are impossible when these intentions are not commonly understood and shared. If I know how you intend to act, given a particular precipitating event, I know how you *will* act.[24] If I know how you will act, I can adjust my actions, not only to the problem at hand but to your likely response to it as well. Simultaneously you will be attempting to anticipate and accommodate my likely actions. Since both of our intentions are anchored in a sense of common purpose, our actions will reinforce and complement one another and produce extremely high levels of coordinated effort and achievement.

In the next section I present a new tool for building shared meaning and mutually recognized interdependence. It is called the *shared intentions process.*

The Shared Intentions Process: Tools for Remaking Strategy

The tools that we use for remaking strategy must build shared meaning and mutually recognized interdependence. Therefore, they must implement the actions—the critical change factors—of achieving through collaboration, humanizing the vision, realizing hidden meaning, and building shared intentions that are necessary for this purpose. Since all of these actions depend on collaboration and sharing for creating meaningful common purposes and intentions, I call the tool for achieving this the *shared intentions process.*

The shared intentions process, like the other concepts and tools in this book, has its roots in both theory and practice. It draws upon a number of disparate sources—from military strategy and psychology, for example—to produce an integrated approach for remaking strategy and implementing the concepts and actions advocated above.

There is extensive literature on processes for strategic planning.[25,26] Various authors have discussed whether planning should be top-down, bottom-up, or some combination of both.[27] Most of these approaches advocate some process within which top management sets goals and then "cascades" these goals down to those at lower levels, who then engage in further planning to implement them.[28] Long-term "strategic" goals are broken down into shorter-term objectives and tactics for achieving them.

Despite the rationality of this process, it does not accomplish the actions that are called for above. Management sets the long-term objectives for the firm with little real input from below. Managers and workers at lower levels participate, but predominantly about "how" to do things and not about "what" things to do. It also tends to be a relatively sterile process, emphasizing objectives and measures with little human content. The sharing of objectives that does take place, takes place almost exclusively within the hierarchical chains of command used to centralize the planning process.

With little human content and with top-management ownership of most important goals, this process does not humanize the vision. Centralization of planning discussions within hierarchical channels limits the possibility of creating a sense of achieving through collaboration. Since only a few people are involved, most people will not participate in strategy discussions and therefore only a few will fully understand the hidden meaning of the strategies that are developed, or recognize their mutual interdependence with others for achieving it. With this sort of process, there can therefore be little shared meaning or mutually recognized interdependence as I have discussed it.

Obviously these processes need to change to implement the concepts and actions recommended above. The shared intentions process accomplishes this by merging ideas from two very separate streams of management thinking—military strategy and psychology. The key idea from military strategy is the concept of "commander's intentions." It allows us to humanize the strategy process, ensures that the strategy is meaningful, and emphasizes intentions as opposed to actions. It results in a meaningful and flexible strategy for those involved in the process. The second concept extends the notion of group coordination through "linking pins,"[29] to widen participation and take the commander's intentions process out of an exclusively hierarchical focus. This encourages lateral (in addition to hierarchical) sharing of intentions. These two processes are integrated and then extended to create a new tool—the shared intentions process—for implementing the actions required for remaking strategy. The next sections discuss and modify the commander's intentions and linking pin concepts for this purpose.

Commander's Intentions

"Commander's intentions" is a very interesting concept from military strategy that helps avoid some of the limitations of conventional strategic planning processes. During the planning of the D-Day invasion in World War II, it became apparent that conventional military planning techniques would not work. Part of the strategy was to have massive numbers of troops parachute behind enemy lines. Once they had landed, it seemed likely that their ability to communicate with one another would be severely limited. How could they coordinate their activities? The answer that was devised was the idea of commander's intentions.

The commander's intentions process required each commander to write down what he intended to do—in this case, after landing behind enemy lines. This was to be written in the first person and confined to one or two pages. It might say something like "After landing, I intend to move my troops to the west to establish a base of operations in the town of Rouen. After accomplishing this, I will use this secure base of operations to begin to drive toward Berlin," and so on.

There are several interesting things about this first step in the commander's intentions process. First, it is written in the first person, and is therefore not dehumanized. Saying that *I* will do something personalizes the process and increases meaning. Second, it focuses on what I *intend* to do. This is a lot different from describing in abstract detail the objectives of what will be done. While intentions and objectives may seem quite similar, they actually have very different behavioral implications. *Intentions are the reasons behind our objectives.* If I know that you intend to establish a base at Rouen in order to allow you to have a secure position from which to move on to Berlin, it helps me to adjust when things do not go as planned. Your *intention* to move to Berlin from a secure base is what is important. Securing Rouen is less so. For example, if I discover that you have been unable to secure Rouen, I still know that your intentions are to move to Berlin from a secure base. I can then anticipate the actions that you might take for this purpose and adjust *my* actions to support yours. If all I know are your goals—establish a base at Rouen—and not your intentions—a secure base from which to move toward Berlin—I cannot manage my contribution to this process as effectively.

Once the commander's intentions have been written, they are then shared with immediate subordinates, who then complete the same process. They write their intentions in support of those of their superior, again in the first person. This process continues down the organization. Each leader is required to understand the intentions of those two levels above them in the hierarchy.

This understanding produces a set of intentions that are shared *within the chain of command.* For a large organization, it is obviously impossible for everyone to know everything that everyone else knows, even if we restrict this to knowledge about strategy. The question then becomes who must share understandings of strategic intent. The commander's intentions process requires that *I* know what *you* intend to do in support of *your superior's* strategy.

Having two levels of strategic understanding is consistent with what we have learned about what constitutes the "top" of the organization.[30] Empirically, when people complete surveys in which they are asked to respond to questions like "In this organization, management . . .," management equals those people who are two levels above them. This is consistent with the commander's intentions rule (two levels of strategic understanding) that establishes the boundaries within which strategy must be shared.

The Limits of Commander's Intentions

The commander's intentions process is very powerful for producing shared meaning. It humanizes the strategy, makes clear the connection to higher purposes that allows achieving through collaboration, and engages levels of the hierarchy in discussions that realize any hidden meaning in the vision. However, the process is still too concentrated in the hierarchy to achieve mutually recognized interdependence.

Most of the sharing and recognition of interdependence that take place, take place *within* the hierarchy. And it is still too top down. This fails to model the boundaryless, process focus, and collaboration dimensions of the adaptive culture. The consistency that is derived is a little like the legislated consistency and negotiated consistency discussed under Stage I and II thinking above. Although commander's intentions is an improvement on earlier thinking, it stops short of our goal. Achieving mutually recognized interdependence requires *lateral* and *vertical* sharing of intentions. This means not only that subordinates and process partners have intentions communicated to them, but that they are actively engaged in a process of influencing the intentions and, in so doing, ensuring a consensus concerning them. This process must be lateral as well as vertical. We need an additional concept for this second purpose, and paradoxically the necessary complement to military thinking can be found in psychology.

Shared Intentions and the "Arc of Understanding"

Commander's intentions shares intentions *within* the hierarchy. We must also share them *laterally*. Some of the actions that were taken in earlier steps for engaging systems and reforming structures have already begun this process. Strategic process workshops, for example, were used to increase lateral process understanding and to manage more effectively on this basis. The outcomes of these workshops were then used at the reforming structures stage as a basis for forming departments in the debureaucratization model. People who were the most interdependent were grouped together. Since lateral interdependence must be recognized in order to form departments, the actions taken for engaging systems and reforming structures build upon one another to create a foundation of mutually recognized interdependence. The previous steps in the *MegaChange* process therefore start the process for building shared meaning and mutually recognized interdependence.

Sharing Intentions Laterally: The "Arc of Understanding"

We have a chance to build upon this foundation at the remaking strategy stage. Using the commander's intentions process not only helps us to make the strategy more meaningful, it adds the concept of intentions to our process understanding. Shared intentions means recognizing our interdependence at a deeper level, not only in terms of the goals we commit to accomplish, but also in terms of the intentions that make those goals meaningful.

Commander's intentions specified the number of levels of hierarchy within which intentions need to be shared. A similar question is raised when we attempt to share intentions laterally as opposed to hierarchically. How extensive should this sharing be? I propose that *everyone must understand the intentions of everyone within two process steps of their position,* in addition to the hierarchical understanding required by the commander's intentions process. This means that each person must understand the intentions of seven positions in the organization: those of the two process steps to the "left" of their position, the two to the "right," those of the two hierarchical levels above them, and their own, as shown in Figure 6.1. This arc of understanding defines the region of mutually recognized interdependence, and defines the zone within which people should attempt to behave in a boundaryless fashion.

Figure 6.1
The "Arc of Understanding"

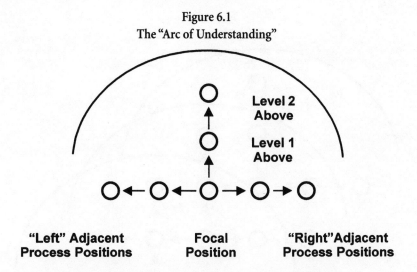

Boundaryless Behavior Occurs Within Arc

Limiting the arc of understanding to seven positions is important due to limitations of human cognition. Research suggests that we can hold in our memory the "magic number 7, ± 2," ideas or categories.[31] Beyond this the information becomes unwieldy for even the best of us. Since we can't understand everything, we have to decide what is the most important. Clearly, we need to understand the intentions of those we report to as well as those of other people who depend on us and on whom we depend. Fortunately this is "doable" by using the rule advanced above.

More Leadership, Less Management

The arc of understanding doesn't leave out subordinates. It includes them in the process of developing our understanding of our own position and our responsibilities to others. Once we have involved our subordinates in shaping our intentions (along with others) and

Figure 6.2
Building Shared Intentions

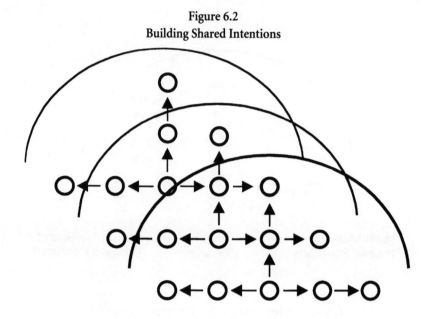

Interlocking Arcs Produce Shared Understanding

a consensus has been reached, the subordinates continue the process of shared intentions from the perspective of *their* positions. They develop their intentions in such a way that their actions are meaningful and consistent with those of *their* management and *their* process colleagues, with collaboration from *their* subordinates. In essence, they become the focal point for a new, overlapping arc of understanding, as shown in Figure 6.2. This arc defines the region within which they must understand and support the critical intentions of the others who are the most relevant to them in developing and implementing the redirected strategy of the firm.

Managers must understand that they do not need (or want) *detailed* knowledge of all the activities of their subordinates. If the process described above has been followed, subordinates will be directing their efforts toward supporting yours. You will have an understanding of the major initiatives being taken to support your mission. However, you no longer need detailed knowledge of each and everyone's specific plans so that you can use it to produce legislated consistency, as in earlier, Stage I or II thinking. Knowledge-based empowerment means that subordinates, understanding the intentions of their management and those of adjacent steps in the core process they operate, have the best knowledge of critical interdependencies *at their level*, and that you should leave them alone to exercise this knowledge. This is fortunate because it would be impossible for you to have this detailed knowledge of everyone's activities anyway.

Why do we consistently fail at micro-management? In debureaucratized structures with wider spans of control, each manager may have as many as 30 to 50 direct reports. It will be difficult for any person to understand all of the detailed plans of the individuals in so large a group (as the "magic number" rule indicates). If we extend this, and require that they also need to know the specific goals of the subordinates of each of their 50 direct reports (using the commander's intentions rule downward), the task clearly becomes impossible. Even in traditional bureaucracies where spans of control average 6 persons, to monitor the actions of 6 direct reports and the 6 subordinates of each of these positions would require that we comprehend 42 sets of goals [(those of 6 subordinates) + (6 × 6 intentions of *their* subordinates) = 42]! This is clearly impossible in the context of debureaucratized structures and wider spans of control, and it renders legislated consistency and micro-management unmanageable and impossible.

Fortunately, the shared intentions process allows us to manage this difficult problem. Using shared intentions, managers *lead* by developing their intentions in the form of a mission, vision, and strategy for their area of responsibility and allowing others to share in shaping them. In older forms of management, managers *manage* the affairs of their subordinates by actively intervening in their day-to-day activities. There is a fundamental distinction between leading and managing in this sense. In the future we will need more leaders and fewer managers. This will be a difficult transition for many who have been brought up to believe that success in organizations is based on being able to tell others what to do. Managers who cling to this old command-and-control notion are likely to be the least successful in the future, for all of the reasons advanced above. Remaking strategy requires more leadership and less management.

Summary

This chapter has introduced a set of concepts, actions, and tools for remaking strategy. We began by reviewing and critiquing earlier stages of evolution of the strategy concept. The first two stages were termed the formulation and formation stages. Although formation ideas improved upon formulation thinking, they shared many of the same limiting and dysfunctional assumptions. In particular, these older approaches were shown to be inadequate for achieving the three functions of any strategy—motivation, direction, and control—in the context of new organizational forms and an empowered workforce.

Stage I and II thinking emphasized the use of goals and consistency among goals for achieving motivation, direction, and coordination. Although these are steps in the right direction, they do not achieve the full potential of these concepts. At the remaking strategy stage of change, *shared meaning* replaces shared goals, and *mutually recognized interdependence* replaces goal consistency. These ideas emphasize intentions and consensus, as opposed to goals and consistency. Intentions are the *reasons* behind goals. Consensus means that we *share* an understanding of each other's goals. Intentions and consensus are more powerful concepts for producing motivation, direction, and coordination.

Shared meaning is produced by actions that allow *achieving through collaboration, humanizing the vision,* and *realizing hidden meaning.* Mutually recognized interdependence is achieved by actions that produce an understanding of *shared intentions.*

The tool for accomplishing both of these objectives is the *shared intentions process,* which is based on concepts from military strategy and psychology. In this process, strategies are developed so that they are based upon the intentions of others who are above and adjacent to us in a managerial and process sense. Subordinates develop their intentions within conceptually similar "arcs of understanding." *Leading* means constantly communicating intentions to, and allowing them to be shaped by, subordinates as well as process colleagues. *They* then follow a similar process to design their own strategies for supporting these shared intentions. Leaders actively avoid interfering in subordinates' work as a way of managing their behavior. Managing in this sense was shown to be impossible in the context of de-layered organizations and wider spans of control due to basic limits of human understanding.

This chapter concludes the second major portion of this book. Segment I introduced the basic assumptions of the book, outlined the stages of organization, and developed the *MegaChange* model, including its cultural dimensions. Segment II discussed each of the four major elements of the model—empowering the workforce, engaging systems, reforming structures, and remaking strategy. This chapter discussed the last of these four steps and returned us to the concept of strategy that launched the first discussion of this segment.

I now turn to the final segment of the book, "Achieving *MegaChange.*" The final chapter in this segment illustrates how each of the steps in the *MegaChange* process—discussed separately up to this point—combine with and complement one another to create true cultural change.

Achieving *MegaChange*

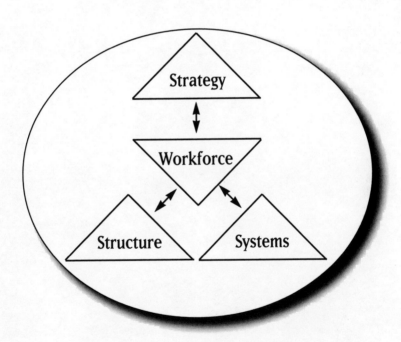

CHAPTER 7

Achieving Cultural Change

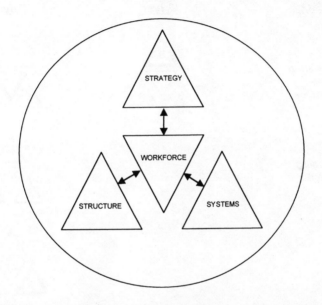

The first segment of this book presented the assumptions and logic of *MegaChange* and introduced the basic change model. The second segment developed each step in the process in detail, focusing on the concepts, actions, and tools that are appropriate at each step. This chapter begins the third portion of the book—"Achieving *MegaChange*"—and deals with the overall orchestration of the transformation process. This chapter presents the change process in its entirety, and it highlights and explains the critical connections between the transformation steps that were discussed separately in Chapters 3 through 6.

The discussion begins with a more rigorous development of the top-down–bottom-up change process that was briefly introduced in Chapter 2. This allows us to build on the useful distinction between organizational transitions and transformations, and to make the

Figure 7.1

Parallel Model of Top-Down–Bottom-Up Change

Transformation Step	Management Driven	Workforce Driven
_1_ **_Empowering the Workforce_**		
_2_ **_Engaging Systems_**		
_3_ **_Reforming Structures_**	 	
_4_ **_Remaking Strategy_**		

point that *MegaChange* is fundamentally a method for achieving transformation and transition *simultaneously*. Weaker methods of change like restructuring and reengineering focus only on transition and often fail to make fundamental and radical change[1] in organizational functioning and performance, as described in Chapter 1.

The *MegaChange* model is then applied to an integrative case. This highly innovative organizational change effort represents what was a leading-edge example of successful transformation and illustrates many of the important concepts of *MegaChange*. The final sections summarize the lessons learned from the "adaptive organization" experience and apply them to the *MegaChange* model.

MegaChange: Applying the New Logic of Change

This book is based upon the belief that it is more appropriate to focus on human capabilities than on limitations when designing and changing organizations. Chapter 2 used this "capability" assumption as a basis for evaluating the first two stages of modern organizations—bureaucracy (Stage I) and complex organizations (Stage II). Each of these stages was contrasted in terms of three "logics" that summarized their major features: a logic of configuration, a logic of content, and a logic of change. Bureaucratic and complex forms of organizations were found wanting in terms of these logics, and their failures were utilized to explain why it will be impossible for them to ever achieve the levels of performance and satisfaction that we all desire.

MegaChange utilizes *new* logics of configuration, content, and change for producing the third stage of organizational evolution, one in which enterprises are both higher-performing *and* more human. The key concept in the new logic of change is the top-down–bottom-up change process described briefly in Chapter 2.

The sequence of chapters in Segment II of the book followed the logic of the top-down–bottom-up process. Each chapter corresponded to one of the key steps in the *MegaChange* process, and the chapters were ordered to reflect the top-down–bottom-up change logic. This section presents an "aerial" view of this sequence. It highlights the overall connections among the steps discussed in the earlier chapters, as well as the complementary roles that management (top down) and the workforce (bottom up) must play in the transformation process. When the concepts, actions, and tools described in each of Chapters 3 through 6 are integrated using this logic, the result is the new ways of thinking, acting, and cooperating that embody the *adaptive culture.*

An overview of the steps in *MegaChange* is shown in Figure 7.1. There are four key transformation steps: *empowering the workforce, engaging systems, reforming structures,* and *remaking strategy.* These transformation steps are ordered in the sequence that they were discussed in Chapters 3 through 6, but Figure 7.1 lets us see the overall connections among them more clearly. Various steps in the process are either management- or workforce-driven, and the highlighted component of the model indicates the focus at each step. Some of the stages are expanded to clarify the actual temporal sequence of change activities. This clarification is especially important at the engaging systems and reforming structures stages, where the change activities overlap somewhat.

Empowering the Workforce

The first step in *MegaChange* is *empowering the workforce.* At this stage management is responsible for legitimizing and initiating the transformation process. The workforce-driven aspects of change involve implementation of the action-based workshops described in detail in Chapter 3. These workshops rely upon the two key concepts from Chapter 3: the *method-as-model* principle and the *performance model.* Individuals are engaged in the change process by direct involvement in a series of interventions that model the end state being pursued—the *adaptive culture* described at the end of

Chapter 2. Empowering the workforce is the first step in *MegaChange* because of the confluence of competitive and technological forces, the values imperative, and the capability assumption. Hypercompetition, new technology, and values shifts require change. Change is so complex that it cannot be managed without the productive engagement of a capable workforce. Empowering this workforce is therefore a necessary first step before it can be involved in helping to design changes in systems, structures, and strategies at latter stages of *MegaChange*.

Engaging Systems

The second step of the top-down–bottom-up process utilizes the newly empowered workforce to begin redesigning key organizational practices and procedures like reward and appraisal systems, reports, meetings, approvals, and other "controls." The critical concept at this step is the *knowledge-based empowerment* principle, which simply says that those with the most knowledge of the problems at hand should be the ones that design changes to address them. Since the workforce operates key systems, they are the ones with the most intimate knowledge of them, and as a consequence they are the ones who should redesign them.

Figure 7.1 indicates that the *engaging systems* stage focuses primarily on the types of systems changes indicated above. There are, however, also some "local" changes in structures at this stage. We might find, for example, that a changed system requires slight changes in staffing to implement it, that a current process has no "owner" in the structure, or that two groups that must coordinate to make a particular system work well are not located near one another. Small, local adjustments in reporting relationships, physical location, or staffing are necessary, and these structural changes can appropriately be workforce-driven because of the workforce's superior knowledge of these issues.

Engaging systems follows empowering the workforce because without empowerment the workforce could not be productively engaged in designing systems change. It precedes reforming structures because large-scale structural change requires redesigned systems and processes as a basis for organizational design. The critical actions at the engaging systems stage are predominantly workforce-driven, as shown in Figure 7.1.

Reforming Structures

The third transformation step in *MegaChange* is *reforming structures*. Reforming structures highlights the consistency criteria that must be satisfied at each step of *MegaChange*: to *support* the firm's strategy and business objectives, to *enable* the previous steps in the change process, and to *model* the desired future. Transitions like restructuring and reengineering usually meet only the support requirement, whereas a true transformation must meet all of them.

Structural changes must support strategy while enabling the process improvements and workforce empowerment begun at earlier steps in *MegaChange*. A structural change that supports a firm's business objectives but is inconsistent with its intended future culture and previous transformation steps is unsatisfactory. Failure to meet this criterion is obvious in reengineering attempts to empower the workforce by "buying people off" or "warehousing" those whose skills are no longer needed. The same is true of Quality efforts that attempt to debureaucratize an organization by simultaneously building a huge bureaucracy of "Quality" managers to manage the process! Everyone knows how silly this is, and everyone knows that it doesn't work.

Reforming structures removes structural barriers that would hinder an empowered workforce and improved, intelligent systems and processes. The key concept for reforming structures is the *debureaucratization model*. The debureaucratization model takes the new processes designed at the engaging systems stage as a starting point for organization design activities. Key processes suggest how people should be grouped to form departments and then, in turn, the rules for coordinating these departments, levels of hierarchy for resolving exceptions to these rules, and the maximum spans of control for managers. Each step depends directly upon the earlier ones. Hence, if the processes that form the beginning for reforming structures are wrong, everything else in the process is wrong as well, and to an increasing degree! Reforming structures therefore must follow engaging systems in the model.

Reforming structures is management-driven according to the knowledge-based empowerment principle. Just as the workforce is most knowledgeable about systems and processes (because it is their job to operate them), management is most knowledgeable about how to manage and design the overall organization. Therefore, they are the key designers of structure, using the expert input they receive as a consequence of earlier actions for engaging systems.

Management also plays a role in designing systems changes, as described in detail in Chapter 5. After having changed overall structures, it is usually necessary to make some organization-wide changes in systems to support them. Thus, while systems changes are primarily workforce-driven, there are also some important changes that are management-led at the reforming structures step of *MegaChange*.

Remaking Strategy

The final step in *MegaChange* is *remaking strategy*. The core concept for remaking strategy is the *shared intentions process*. This is the last step because accomplishing each of the preceding steps is a necessary precondition for humanizing and creating more meaningful and productive organizations. A meaningful strategy is impossible without empowerment, legitimate work, and structures that allow achievement. Those who labor in controlling, manipulative, and limiting environments cannot envision a better future because their vision is constrained by their current position. Unfortunately, many believe this to be the necessary reality of organizational life. The first three steps of *MegaChange* give us a vantage point from which to create our own *desirable* future. The processes for remaking strategy resolve the dilemmas that we must face in getting there and produce a meaningful vision that embodies the destination that we seek.

Remaking strategy is both management- *and* workforce-driven because the strategies that are developed are jointly developed. They allow collaborative achievement, humanize the vision, and allow each person to perceive the strategy as meaningful. Using the shared intentions process, everyone participates in creating strategy, not just a managerial elite or specialized staff units.

Key Features of the Top-Down–Bottom-Up Logic

This new logic of change has a number of key features. First, the process is not top down or bottom up; it is *both*. This is highlighted in Figure 7.1 by focusing on the Management-Driven and Workforce-Driven columns. When we look only at the sequence of management-driven changes, the highlighted elements of the basic model appear in a sequence that is clearly top down. Management legitimates the change (strategy), debureaucratizes the structure (structure), designs large-scale systems to support the new organization (systems), and then co-creates the future strategy with the workforce (returning to strategy). The sequence is the normal *transition* or implementation sequence: strategy-structure-systems.

When we focus on the Workforce-Driven column, the opposite is true. The workforce first concentrates on empowerment and then redesigns and simplifies key processes (systems), eliminates unnecessary rules and makes local changes in work assignments and staffing (structures), and finally co-creates the future strategy of the firm with management (strategy). The sequence is *transformational:* steps are taken to create an empowered workforce that first addresses systems, then structures, and finally strategies. Each step in this bottom-up process directly produces *new* ways of thinking, acting, and cooperating—the three key dimensions of the adaptive culture.

The process described above extends over several years and is *neither* top down nor bottom up as I have described it. It is actually both, and it requires very close coordination, not only between the steps in each sequence (strategy, structure, and systems) but also between the two management- and workforce-driven sequences themselves. Therefore, the consistency criteria that were applied at each step of the overall *MegaChange* process—to support, enable and model—and which were highlighted in the discussion of reforming structures above, are vitally important.

Every step in the process shown in Figure 7.1 must meet these criteria, regardless of whether the step is one that is predominantly management- or workforce-driven. This requirement is seen most clearly in the case of the reforming structures stage, because at this point it is very clear that whatever changes are made must simultaneously support the organization's strategic objectives with respect to competition and enable earlier steps in cultural transformation. Organizations in *MegaChange* must maneuver to address changing competitive forces (transition) while simultaneously building a better organization and culture for the future (transformation). This requires an articulated top-down–bottom-up change process that emphasizes both transition and transformation, and in which each step supports strategic objectives, enables previous steps in the change process, and models the desired future. As managers at the General Electric Company put it: "We have to change the tires while the car is moving!" This is the process for achieving that objective.

Achieving Cultural Change:
The "Adaptive Organization" Project

Some of the ideas presented above are necessarily rather abstract. The purpose of this section is to illustrate the *MegaChange* model by reporting the results of an exemplary change effort that was undertaken by a division of a major corporation. The case explains many of the important features of *MegaChange* by example, and clearly depicts the overall sequence of the change process.

Background

The Adaptive Organization project (AO) was initiated in the operations unit of a division of the company by the manager of operations.

The operations unit was a highly diverse unit in terms of the technical specialities that it contained. It was responsible for a number of both traditional and nontraditional operations activities. The operations unit managed plant and equipment, data centers, and plant maintenance. Because of the high-technology nature of their product, equipment needs were quite sophisticated. The workforce contained approximately 400 people, who ranged in education from high school graduates to Ph.D. computer scientists.

The end of the Cold War had reduced the demand for the company's products. Ronald Reagan left the presidency, and some in the industry said that "the customer retired and went home to California." With these events, the competitive and political environment had radically changed in less than two years' time. With less demand, the entire industry was faced with overcapacity and the difficult problem of turning specialized expertise to new applications.

The operations unit was not immune to these pressures. The division faced a need to reduce its operating budget by approximately $3 million. One way to accomplish this was through downsizing, but the organization had already been through a number of reorganizations that had reduced critical resources. That made this option unattractive. Finding another way of addressing this competitive threat seemed desirable.

The manager of operations was widely viewed by those he worked with as a person who got things done, had a good rapport with his staff, and had been a leader in recent large-scale change efforts aimed at empowering the workforce. He believed that it was time to fundamentally alter the way the operations unit was organized and managed.

After a short period of study, he implemented the Adaptive Organization concept within operations. Its main features were:

1. A radical delayering of the organization's structure. Prior to the change there were at least seven layers of management within the unit, some of which were "unofficial," but which were there nonetheless. Following the change there were two levels.
2. Teams were formed around key processes, replacing the functional work units that had existed in the past.
3. Process leaders were appointed to manage these processes, and they were the only formal managers in the new structure. Each process manager managed a set of process teams.
4. Former managers who were not appointed process leaders became team members. The teams elected their own leaders. Some of these leaders were the former functional managers and some were not.
5. The teams were given significant discretion to manage their own activities.
6. An intensive training program was launched to train the teams and the process managers in the skills necessary to function in the new organization. The process managers received a short course in team skills from internal consultants, and immediately following this they trained their teams. Everyone in the organi-

zation received training within four weeks of the beginning of the new structure.

The initial implementation of the Adaptive Organization was predominantly a structural change. However, it occurred in the context of a much broader transformation that encompassed all four of the steps of the *MegaChange* model. The following sections describe this overall change process in detail. At each step of the process, I summarize the actions that were taken, the results that were achieved, and the challenges that led to the next step in the process. The Adaptive Organization program was remarkable when viewed in this context because it went so far in the change process. The results were also remarkable, as we shall see.

Empowering the Workforce

Prior to the implementation of the changes in structure discussed above, the operations unit had been heavily involved in workforce empowerment activites. One of the primary methods for achieving change were meetings, at which people were encouraged to find new ways of reducing bureaucracy, eliminating unnecessary work, and improving performance. Managers listened to action plans developed by the workforce and were required to respond to them.

Within the operations unit, numerous productive changes were initiated based upon these meetings. *Every* member of the unit attended at least one empowerment session, and many attended more. The manager of operations was a visible champion of the process.

There are a number of important points to be made here. First, top management at the organization legitimized and emotionally supported the empowerment effort. There were significant resources dedicated to the change process, and it was explicitly tied to the strategy of the organization. Top management played the key role that it must play in initiating the empowering the workforce step of *MegaChange,* as described in detail in Chapter 3.

From the workforce perspective, the empowerment change process followed the method-as-model principle. The meetings were a microcosm of how the organization was intended to operate in the future. They also were consistent with the performance model. Everyone was directly involved in an empowering experience, rather than being told that they had been "empowered." This produced a *motivation* to participate due to the motivational factors discussed at length in Chapter 3. Managers modeled the desired changes in relationships between supervisors and subordinates, increasing *understanding,* as everyone demonstrated, practiced, and refined new ways of acting. Based upon these experiences and with the help of a change council, the workforce developed its *ability* to act in these new ways. All three ingredients for changed behavior were there: new motivations, abilities, and job understanding. The result was widespread empowered behavior within the workforce of the operations unit.

Workforce approval of the change process was very high. Surveys indicated that 94 percent of the workforce rated the change process as either "very successful" or "excellent."

Engaging Systems

The first step in the change process had been remarkably successful. At the time that these efforts were initiated, there were over a dozen other change "projects" under way, several of which had purposes similar to those of the empowerment process. By the end of the first six months of the effort, all of these competing initiatives had been incorporated into the change process due to its overwhelming success.

Approximately one year into the process the topics of the workshops began to focus more on processes than on the general issues that had occupied them most of the first year. The workforce was not content to confine their work to their immediate jobs, and wanted to improve the processes that they were responsible for. Change activities became more topical and business-focused, and results continued to improve.

These efforts paralleled the widespread emergence of reengineering as a methodology for improving business processes. It is important that the efforts reported here were driven by the organization members themselves. Only one outside consultant was involved, and that individual did not attempt to introduce any new or specific methodologies for process mapping or improvement. The model was simply to engage an empowered workforce in the process of rethinking their policies, procedures, and processes and give them ownership of the responsibility for improving them.

More and more problems were resolved and more and more people were involved in multiple sessions of the workshops. Cultural change was under way. And then a peculiar thing happened. People began to become disenchanted with the change process, even as it continued to make sustained improvements in organizational performance. People who had been confirmed supporters of the process began to have doubts. The change effort had "hit the wall" in the sense described in Chapter 3, and for many of the reasons described there.

The first two steps of the *MegaChange* process had been very successfully implemented. However, it was becoming more and more apparent that there were limits to the gains that could be made by confining change to only the workforce level. Certainly, significant gains had been made in changing some human resource practices, but these were small in comparison to those that could be made if the organization were to take the next steps toward reforming structures.

New processes were constrained by old structures. Empowered behaviors were stifled by too many levels of hierarchy. Managerial behavior had changed less than workforce behavior. The workforce had been working overtime, transforming their culture while simultaneously meeting the demands of a constantly shifting and hyper-competitive environment. It was clear that there needed to be a next step, but it was unclear what that step should be.

Reforming Structures

Operations now faced the situation described under the "Background" section above. There was tremendous pressure on the unit to continue to perform at higher and higher levels. Over $3 million had to be eliminated from the operating budget, and they did not want to accomplish this with layoffs. The manager of operations knew that the first steps in change had been very successful, but they were now entering a new stage where what had worked before would no longer be effective at the same level. The workforce had changed, but structures and strategies had not.

In response to these forces, the manager of operations implemented the Adaptive Organization. The major features of the AO concept are explained above. The team leaders were initially assigned their roles, but shortly into the change the team members requested that they be allowed to select their own leaders. Some of these transitions were very painful, but as the change proceeded the teams continued to take on more and more self-management. Teams were formed around core processes, and the intention was for these teams to perform in a boundaryless way. Large-scale training helped team members to learn how to function in the new environment. The move to the Adaptive Organization was consistent with the *debureaucratization model* described in Chapter 5. The move to restructure operations was undertaken only after they had developed a strong understanding of their core processes at the engaging systems stage described above.

Approximately six months into the change, the consultant conducted extensive interviews to assess the progress of the change. From a performance standpoint, things were progressing well. The

$3 million budget reduction had been accomplished without any layoffs. Everyone was challenged by the new structure, and it raised some new issues that had never existed before: How should performance appraisals be handled? What does a career mean in an organization that has no hierarchy? Now that I am not a manager anymore, what is my future with this organization? These are precisely the dilemmas of debureaucratization that have been discussed in earlier chapters.

Responding to these questions required some large-scale systems change within the operations unit.[2] Again, these changes were made by members of the organization themselves. Staff assistance was used very sparingly. The idea was that it was up to the people who had to live with the systems to design them. A new performance appraisal and pay delivery system was put in place that was consistent with the new structure. The Adaptive Organization concept implemented fundamental structural change and debureaucratization to *enable* earlier changes in systems and empowerment to proceed. It also *supported* the business objectives of the operations unit. Reducing layers and the boundaries between managers and workers also *modeled* the desired future culture.

Remaking Strategy

Following this, the consultant conducted another set of extensive interviews and analyses within the operations unit. As he had performed a similar study for the organization earlier, he was able to assess the progress they were making and what new challenges they faced as the transformation process continued. The first finding was that the workforce was becoming more and more interested in the overall vision and structure of the organization. At the reforming structures stage, concerns about structure had been very *local* (How should the new process teams be organized? What are our roles and responsibilities?). By now these issues had been largely resolved and people were working at integrating the *overall* structure of teams. The questions were becoming more strategic (Are these the right teams? How should cross-team coordination be handled?).

Similarly, the early concerns with strategy were around what the goals of the Adaptive Organization changes were. Now these were no longer an issue. Everyone was interested in creating a new vision for *operations,* not just for the change. The new vision would be one that reflected operations' accomplishments in empowerment, process focus, debureaucratization, and change management and included input from everyone.

This finding illustrates a point made above in the discussion of the "aerial" view of the *MegaChange* process. Operations would not—perhaps *could* not—be considering a radical new vision if it had not taken the first three steps in the change process described above. New experiences of empowerment, revitalized systems and processes, and debureaucratized structures provided a vantage point for a new strategy that would not have been imaginable outside the context of change described here.

In the aftermath of several mergers, the organization has undergone a good deal of refinement and realignment, some of which has directly impacted the structure of the operations unit. While it is no longer known as the Adaptive Organization, its employees, both past and present, have maintained their passion for this type of structure. As a result, most of the values, principles and systems that were integral to the Adaptive Organization remain very much alive and, in fact, are taking root within other areas of the organization.

As a transformation, the Adaptive Organization effort was successful. There was a cultural change within the organization, which resulted in new ways of thinking, acting, and cooperating. And, although the cultural change has not followed all of the prescriptions of the *MegaChange* process presented in the preceding chapters, it did illustrate the core concepts and sequence of the model, as shown in Figure 7.2.

Figure 7.2
The Adaptive Organization Transformation

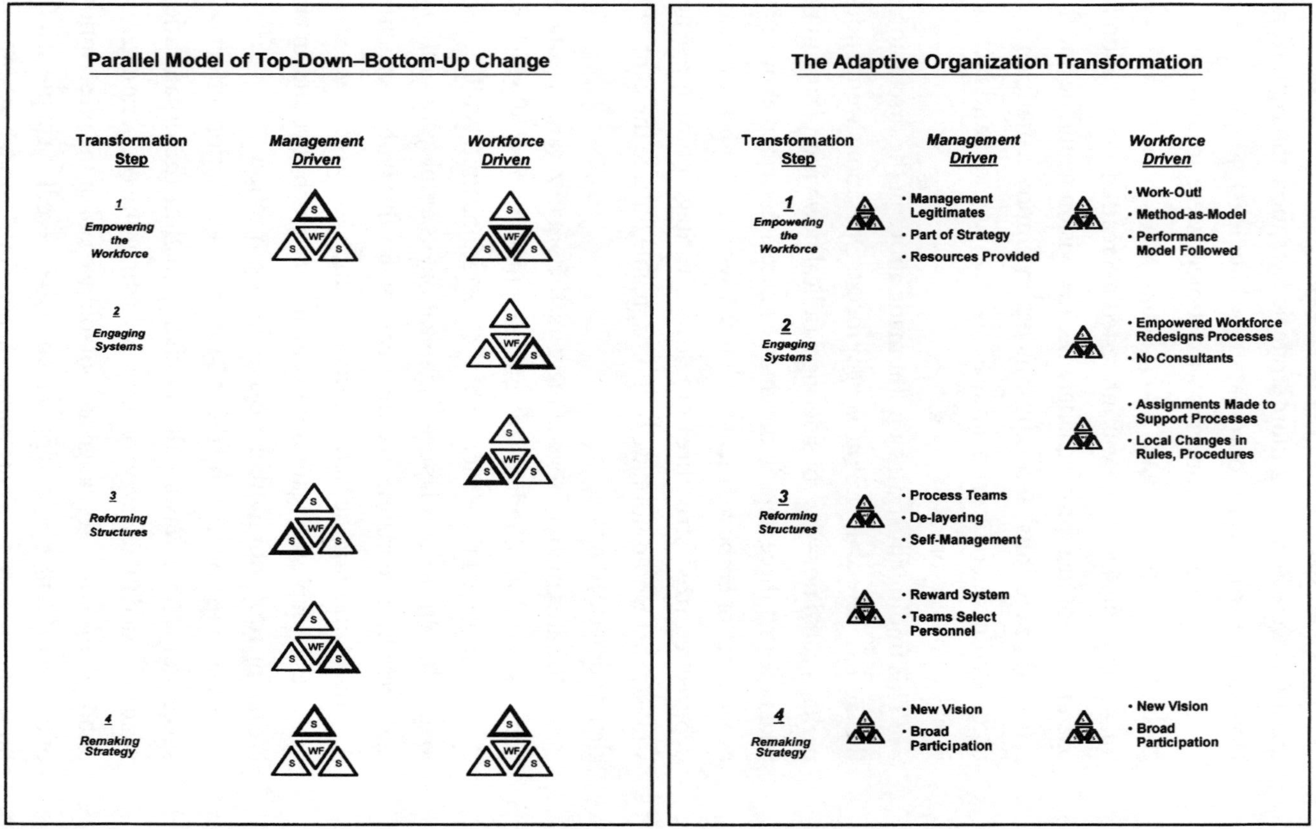

Summary and Conclusions

At this time many organizations are still attempting to make restructuring and reengineering work. They will not be successful because these efforts are merely transitional and not transformational. The forces for change described in Chapter 1 make it clear that transitions within Stage I and Stage II organizational forms cannot respond to the constellation of competitive, technological, and values imperatives that characterize the current environment. A total, system-wide cultural transformation to Stage III organizations is necessary. The Adaptive Organization effort is an excellent example of how these changes can be made.

This chapter has illustrated the overall process of *MegaChange*. The process is built upon the capability assumption and the belief that organizations should aspire to a higher standard of performance than that embodied in conventional financial performance criteria. The concepts, actions, and tools of *MegaChange* draw selectively from research and practice in strategic management, psychology, organizational behavior and theory, and management. They work with one another to support, enable, and model the development of a new organizational form.

MegaChange takes a long time, certainly longer than managers concerned with a quick fix would like it to take. It requires a committed and visionary leader who is constantly involved throughout the change. It is not for managers who would like to delegate responsibility for change to others, or buy it from consultants. It won't be over by the next quarter. But, unlike change methods that promise radical change in short time frames with little of your involvement, *it works.* That is enough.

Notes

Chapter 1

1. March, James G., and Herbert A. Simon. *Organizations.* New York: John Wiley and Sons, 1958.
2. Fichte, Johann Gottlieb. "The Vocation of Man," in William Smith, ed., *The Popular Works of Johann Gottleib Fichte.* 4th edition. London: Trubner, 1889.
3. Frankl, Viktor. *Man's Search for Meaning: An Introduction to Logotherapy.* Trans. by Ilse Lasch. Boston: Beacon Press, 1963.
4. Lawler, Edward E. *The Ultimate Advantage.* San Francisco: Jossey-Bass, 1992.
5. Peters, Thomas J. *Thriving on Chaos: Handbook for a Management Revolution.* New York: Knopf, 1987.
6. Galbraith, Jay R., and Edward E. Lawler. *Organizing for the Future: The New Logic for Managing Complex Organizations.* San Francisco: Jossey-Bass, 1993.
7. Filipowski, Dianne. "Downsizing Isn't Always Rightsizing," *Personnel Journal,* Nov. 1993, p. 71.
8. Champy, James. *Reengineering Management.* New York: Harper Business, 1995.
9. March, James G., and Herbert A. Simon. *Organizations,* p. 5.
10. D'Aveni, Richard. *Hypercompetition.* New York: The Free Press, 1994.
11. Galbraith, Jay R., and Edward E. Lawler. *Organizing for the Future.*
12. Toffler, Alvin. *Future Shock.* New York: Random House, 1970.
13. Deutschman, Alan. "The Upbeat Generation," *Fortune* 126: 1 (July 13, 1992): pp. 42–48, 52–54.
14. Ludeman, Kate. "From Work Ethic to Worth Ethic," *Executive Excellence,* vol. 6 (1989), pp. 7–8.
15. Kofodimos, Joan. "Why Executives Lose Their Balance," *Organizational Dynamics,* vol. 19 (1990), pp. 58–73.

16. Brown, Thomas L. "Are You Living in 'Quiet Desperation'?" *Industry Week*, vol. 241 (1992), p. 17.

17. Taylor, Frederick. *The Principles of Scientific Management.* New York: Harper and Brothers Publishers, 1911.

18. Kaplan, Abraham. *The Conduct of Inquiry.* New York: Chandler Publishing Co., 1964.

19. Leavitt, Harold. "Applied Organizational Change in Industry: Structural, Technological, and Humanistic Approaches," in James March, ed., *Handbook of Organizations.* Chicago: Rand McNally & Co., 1965.

20. Galbraith, Jay R. *Designing Complex Organizations.* Reading, Mass.: Addison-Wesley, 1973.

21. Hrebiniak, Lawrence G., and William F. Joyce. *Implementing Strategy.* New York: Macmillan, 1984.

Chapter 2

1. Weber, Max. *The Theory of Social and Economic Organization.* Translated by A. M. Henderson and Talcott Parsons. New York: Oxford University Press, 1947.

2. Fayol, Henri. *General and Industrial Management.* Translated by Constance Storrs. London: Pitman Publishing, 1949.

3. Urwick, Lyndall. *The Elements of Administration.* New York: Harper and Bros., 1944.

4. Lawrence, Paul, and Jay Lorsch. "Differentiation and Integration in Complex Organizations," *Administrative Science Quarterly,* vol. 12 (June 1967), pp. 1–47.

5. Galbraith, Jay R. *Designing Complex Organizations.* Boston: Addison-Wesley, 1972.

6. Joyce, William F. "Matrix Organization: A Social Experiment in Planned Change," *Academy of Management Journal* 29:3 (1986), pp. 536–561.

7. Lorange, Peter. *Corporate Planning: An Executive Viewpoint.* Englewood Cliffs, N.J.: Prentice-Hall, 1980.

8. Hrebiniak, Lawrence G., and William F. Joyce. *Implementing Strategy.* New York: Macmillan, 1984.

9. Quinn, James B. *Strategies for Change: Logical Incrementalism.* Homewood, Ill.: Richard D. Irwin, 1980.

10. Schein, Edgar. *Organizational Culture and Leadership.* San Francisco: Jossey-Bass, 1992.

11. Ledford, Gerald. "High-Involvement Work Teams," in Edward E. Lawler, ed., *The Ultimate Advantage.* San Francisco: Jossey-Bass, 1992.

Chapter 3

1. Hammer, Michael, and James Champy. *Re-engineering the Corporation: A Manifesto for Business Revolution.* New York: Harper Business, 1993.
2. Joyce, William. "Towards a Theory of Incrementalism," in Robert Lamb and Paul Shrivastava, eds., *Advances in Strategic Management.* Vol. 4. Greenwich, Conn.: JAI Press, 1986.
3. Wrapp, H. Edward. "Good Managers Don't Make Policy Decisions," *Harvard Business Review,* September, 1967: pp. 91–99.
4. Deming, W. Edwards. *The New Economics for Industry, Government, and Education.* Cambridge, Mass.: MIT Center for Advanced Engineering Study, 1993.
5. Lewin, Kurt. "Frontiers of Group Dynamics," *Human Relations,* Vol 1 (1947), pp. 5–41.
6. Campbell, John P., and Robert D. Pritchard. "Motivation Theory in Industrial and Organizational Psychology," in Marvin D. Dunnette, ed., *Handbook of Industrial and Organizational Psychology.* Chicago: Rand McNally, 1976.
7. Lawler, Edward E. *Motivation in Work Organizations,* Belmont, Calif.: Brooks Cole, 1973.
8. Maslow, Abraham H. *Motivation and Personality.* New York: Harper and Row, 1954.
9. Alderfer, Clay P. "An Empirical Test of a New Theory of Human Needs," *Organizational Behavior and Human Performance,* vol. 4 (1969), pp. 142–175.
10. Thompson, Victor. *Modern Organization.* New York: Knopf, 1966.
11. Delbecq, Andre, Andrew H. Van de Ven, and D. H. Gustafson. *Group Techniques for Program Planning: A Guide to Nominal and Delphi Processes.* Glenview, Ill.: Scott, Foresman, 1975, pp. 7–10, 17–18.
12. Lucent Corporation. Annual Report, 1997.
13. Waxler, Carolyn. "A Giant Grower Slows," *Forbes,* December 1, 1997.
14. Personal communication, Craig Gill, Lucent Technologies, August 1998.
15. Lucent Corporation. Annual Report, 1997.

Chapter 4

1. Joyce, William, John Slocum, and Victor McGee. "Designing Lateral Organizations: An Analysis of the Benefits, Costs and Factors Enabling Non-Hierarchical Organizational Forms," *Decision Sciences,* Special Issue on Designing 21st Century Organizations, 1997.
2. Dotlich, David L. and Noel, James L. *Action Learning.* San Francisco, Calif.: Jossey-Bass, 1998.

3. Lawler, Edward E. *Motivation in Work Organizations*. Belmont, Calif. Brooks Cole, 1973.

4. London, Manuel. "360-Degree Feedback as a Competitive Advantage," *Human Resource Management*, Summer, 1993.

5. Campbell, Donald T., and D. W. Fiske. "Convergent and Discriminant Validation by the Multitrait-Multimethod Matrix," *Psychological Bulletin*, vol. 56 (1959), pp. 81–105.

6. Lawler, Edward E. *Pay and Organizational Effectiveness: A Psychological View*. New York: McGraw Hill, 1971.

7. Sonnenfeld, Jeffrey, and John Kotter. "The Maturation of Career Theory," *Human Relations*, vol. 35 (1982), pp. 19–46.

8. Adams, J. S. "Wage Inequities, Productivity, and Work Quality," *Industrial Relations*, vol. 3 (1963), pp. 9–16.

9. Lawler, Edward E. *Strategic Pay: Aligning Organizational Strategies and Pay Systems*. San Francisco: Jossey-Bass, 1990.

Chapter 5

1. Champy, James. *Reengineering Management*. New York: Harper Business, 1995.

2. Hrebiniak, Lawrence G., and William F. Joyce. *Implementing Strategy*. New York: Macmillan, 1984.

3. Ibid.

4. Lawrence, Paul, and Jay Lorsch. "Differentiation and Integration in Complex Organizations," *Administrative Science Quarterly*, vol. 12 (June 1967), pp. 1–47.

5. Hrebiniak, Lawrence G., and William F. Joyce. *Implementing Strategy*. New York: Macmillan, 1984.

6. Galbraith, Jay R. *Designing Complex Organizations*. Boston: Addison-Wesley, 1972.

7. Lawrence, Paul, and Jay Lorsch. "Differentiation and Integration in Complex Organizations."

8. Galbraith, Jay R. *Designing Organizations*. San Francisco: Jossey-Bass, 1995.

9. Schlesinger, Leonard. Unpublished document, Harvard Business School, 1989.

10. Galbraith, Jay R. *Competing with Flexible Lateral Organizations*. 2nd ed. Reading, Mass.: Addison-Wesley, 1994.

11. Hrebiniak, Lawrence G., and William F. Joyce. *Implementing Strategy*.

12. Filipowski, Dianne. "Downsizing Isn't Always Rightsizing," *Personnel Journal*, Nov. 1993, p. 71.

Chapter 3

1. Hammer, Michael, and James Champy. *Re-engineering the Corporation: A Manifesto for Business Revolution.* New York: Harper Business, 1993.

2. Joyce, William. "Towards a Theory of Incrementalism," in Robert Lamb and Paul Shrivastava, eds., *Advances in Strategic Management.* Vol. 4. Greenwich, Conn.: JAI Press, 1986.

3. Wrapp, H. Edward. "Good Managers Don't Make Policy Decisions," *Harvard Business Review,* September, 1967: pp. 91–99.

4. Deming, W. Edwards. *The New Economics for Industry, Government, and Education.* Cambridge, Mass.: MIT Center for Advanced Engineering Study, 1993.

5. Lewin, Kurt. "Frontiers of Group Dynamics," *Human Relations,* Vol 1 (1947), pp. 5–41.

6. Campbell, John P., and Robert D. Pritchard. "Motivation Theory in Industrial and Organizational Psychology," in Marvin D. Dunnette, ed., *Handbook of Industrial and Organizational Psychology.* Chicago: Rand McNally, 1976.

7. Lawler, Edward E. *Motivation in Work Organizations,* Belmont, Calif.: Brooks Cole, 1973.

8. Maslow, Abraham H. *Motivation and Personality.* New York: Harper and Row, 1954.

9. Alderfer, Clay P. "An Empirical Test of a New Theory of Human Needs," *Organizational Behavior and Human Performance,* vol. 4 (1969), pp. 142–175.

10. Thompson, Victor. *Modern Organization.* New York: Knopf, 1966.

11. Delbecq, Andre, Andrew H. Van de Ven, and D. H. Gustafson. *Group Techniques for Program Planning: A Guide to Nominal and Delphi Processes.* Glenview, Ill.: Scott, Foresman, 1975, pp. 7–10, 17–18.

12. Lucent Corporation. Annual Report, 1997.

13. Waxler, Carolyn. "A Giant Grower Slows," *Forbes,* December 1, 1997.

14. Personal communication, Craig Gill, Lucent Technologies, August 1998.

15. Lucent Corporation. Annual Report, 1997.

Chapter 4

1. Joyce, William, John Slocum, and Victor McGee. "Designing Lateral Organizations: An Analysis of the Benefits, Costs and Factors Enabling Non-Hierarchical Organizational Forms," *Decision Sciences,* Special Issue on Designing 21st Century Organizations, 1997.

2. Dotlich, David L. and Noel, James L. *Action Learning.* San Francisco, Calif.: Jossey-Bass, 1998.

3. Lawler, Edward E. *Motivation in Work Organizations.* Belmont, Calif. Brooks Cole, 1973.

4. London, Manuel. "360-Degree Feedback as a Competitive Advantage," *Human Resource Management,* Summer, 1993.

5. Campbell, Donald T., and D. W. Fiske. "Convergent and Discriminant Validation by the Multitrait-Multimethod Matrix," *Psychological Bulletin,* vol. 56 (1959), pp. 81–105.

6. Lawler, Edward E. *Pay and Organizational Effectiveness: A Psychological View.* New York: McGraw Hill, 1971.

7. Sonnenfeld, Jeffrey, and John Kotter. "The Maturation of Career Theory," *Human Relations,* vol. 35 (1982), pp. 19–46.

8. Adams, J. S. "Wage Inequities, Productivity, and Work Quality," *Industrial Relations,* vol. 3 (1963), pp. 9–16.

9. Lawler, Edward E. *Strategic Pay: Aligning Organizational Strategies and Pay Systems.* San Francisco: Jossey-Bass, 1990.

Chapter 5

1. Champy, James. *Reengineering Management.* New York: Harper Business, 1995.

2. Hrebiniak, Lawrence G., and William F. Joyce. *Implementing Strategy.* New York: Macmillan, 1984.

3. Ibid.

4. Lawrence, Paul, and Jay Lorsch. "Differentiation and Integration in Complex Organizations," *Administrative Science Quarterly,* vol. 12 (June 1967), pp. 1–47.

5. Hrebiniak, Lawrence G., and William F. Joyce. *Implementing Strategy.* New York: Macmillan, 1984.

6. Galbraith, Jay R. *Designing Complex Organizations.* Boston: Addison-Wesley, 1972.

7. Lawrence, Paul, and Jay Lorsch. "Differentiation and Integration in Complex Organizations."

8. Galbraith, Jay R. *Designing Organizations.* San Francisco: Jossey-Bass, 1995.

9. Schlesinger, Leonard. Unpublished document, Harvard Business School, 1989.

10. Galbraith, Jay R. *Competing with Flexible Lateral Organizations.* 2nd ed. Reading, Mass.: Addison-Wesley, 1994.

11. Hrebiniak, Lawrence G., and William F. Joyce. *Implementing Strategy.*

12. Filipowski, Dianne. "Downsizing Isn't Always Rightsizing," *Personnel Journal,* Nov. 1993, p. 71.

13. Hrebiniak, Lawrence G., and William F. Joyce. *Implementing Strategy.*
14. Baumohl, Bernard. "Then Downsizing Becomes Dumbsizing," *Industry Week,* January 18, 1993.
15. Kaplan, Abraham. *The Conduct of Inquiry.* New York: Chandler Publishing Co., 1964.
16. Galbraith, Jay R. *Designing Organizations.* San Francisco: Jossey-Bass, 1995.

Chapter 6

1. Lorange, Peter. *Corporate Planning.* Englewood Cliffs, N.J.: Prentice-Hall, Inc. 1980.
2. Porter, Michael E. *Competitive Strategy: Techniques for Analyzing Industries and Competitors.* New York: Free Press, 1985.
3. Peters, Thomas J., and Robert H. Waterman. *In Search of Excellence: Lessons from America's Best Run Companies.* New York: Harper and Row, 1982.
4. Lindblom, Charles E. "The Science of 'Muddling Through,'" *Public Administration Review,* pp. 79–88. July–August (1959).
5. Quinn, James B. *Strategies for Change: Logical Incrementalism.* Homewood, Ill.: Richard D. Irwin, 1980.
6. Quinn, James B., Henry Mintzberg, and Robert M. James. *The Strategy Process: Concepts, Contexts, and Cases.* Englewood Cliffs, N.J.: Prentice-Hall, 1988.
7. Mintzberg, Henry, D. Raisingnani, and A. Theoret. "The Structure of 'Unstructured' Decision Processes," *Administrative Science Quarterly* (1976), pp. 246–275.
8. Nutt, Paul C. "Types of Organizational Decision Processes," *Administrative Science Quarterly* (1984), pp. 414–450.
9. Grandori, Anna. "A Prescriptive Contingency View of Organizational Decision Making," *Administrative Science Quarterly,* vol. 29 (1984), pp. 192–209.
10. Quinn, James B. *Strategies for Change: Logical Incrementalism.*
11. Thompson, Victor. *Modern Organization.* New York: Knopf, 1966, p. 222.
12. Wrapp, H. Edward. "Good Managers Don't Make Policy Decisions," *Harvard Business Review,* September, 1967: pp. 91–99.
13. Hrebiniak, Lawrence G. *The We-Force in Management: How to Build and Sustain Cooperation.* New York: Lexington Books, 1994.
14. Thompson, Victor. *Modern Organization.* New York:
15. Quinn, James B. *Strategies for Change: Logical Incrementalism.*
16. Frankl, Viktor. *Man's Search for Meaning: An Introduction to Logotherapy.* Trans. Ilse Lasch. Boston: Beacon Press, 1963.

17. Fichte, Johann Gottleib. "The Vocation of Man," in William Smith, ed., *The Popular Works of Johann Gottleib Fichte*. 4th edition. London: Trubner, 1889.

18. Joyce, William, and John Slocum. "Collective Climate: Agreement as a Basis for Defining Aggregate Climates in Organizations," *Academy of Management Journal* 27:4 (1984), pp. 1–22.

19. Thompson, Victor. *Modern Organization*.

20. Joyce, William, and John Slocum. "Collective Climate."

21. Herzberg, F., B. Mausner, and B. Snyderman. *The Motivation to Work*. 2nd ed. New York: Wiley, 1959.

22. Hackman, J., and G. Oldham. "Development of the Job Diagnostic Survey," *Journal of Applied Psychology*, vol. 60 (1975), p. 161.

23. Lewin, Kurt. *Principles of Topological Psychology*. New York: McGraw-Hill, 1936.

24. Drucker, Peter F. *The Practice of Management*. New York: Harper, 1954.

25. Steiner, George. *Strategic Planning: What Every Manager Must Know*. New York: Free Press, 1979.

26. Lorange, Peter. *Corporate Planning*. Englewood Cliffs, N.J.: Prentice-Hall, Inc. 1980.

27. Hax, Arnoldo, and Nicolas Majluf. *The Strategy Concept and Process: A Pragmatic Approach*. Upper Saddle River, N.J.: Prentice-Hall, 1996.

28. Hrebiniak, Lawrence G., and William F. Joyce. *Implementing Strategy*. New York: Macmillan, 1984.

29. Likert, Rensis. *New Patterns of Management*. New York: McGraw-Hill, 1961.

30. Hollmann, Thomas. Personal communication based upon studies at the General Electric Corporation.

31. Miller, George A. "The Magical Number Seven, Plus or Minus Two: Some Limits on Our Capacity for Processing Information," *Eastern Psychological Association*, Philadelphia, 1955.

Chapter 7

1. Champy, James. *Reengineering Management*. New York: Harper Business, 1995.

2. Hrebiniak, Lawrence G., and William F. Joyce. *Implementing Strategy*. New York: Macmillan, 1984.

Index